MARY SHELLEY
Frankenstein's Creator

THE BARNARD BIOGRAPHY SERIES

MARY SHELLEY

Frankenstein's Creator

First Science Fiction Writer

—◦◦◦—

Joan Kane Nichols

CONARI PRESS

for my brother, Joe Kane

Copyright © 1998 by Joan Kane Nichols.

All Rights Reserved. No part of this book may be used or reproduced in any manner whatsoever without written permission, except in the case of brief quotations in critical articles or reviews. For information, contact: Conari Press, 2550 Ninth Street, Suite 101, Berkeley, CA 94710-2551.

Conari Press books are distributed by Publishers Group West

ISBN: 1-57324-087-7

Cover design: Suzanne Albertson

Library of Congress Cataloging-in-Publication Data

Nichols, Joan Kane.
  Mary Shelley, Frankenstein's creator : first science fiction writer / by Joan Kane Nichols.
      p.   cm. — (The Barnard biography series)
  Includes bibliographical references. (p. 181).
  Summary: A biography of the nineteenth-century English writer who at the age of nineteen wrote the classic horror novel "Frankenstein."
  ISBN 1–57324–087–7 (trade paper)
  1. Shelley, Mary Wollstonecraft. 1797–1851—Juvenile literature.
  2. Women authors, English—19th century—Biography—Juvenile literature. 3. Frankenstein (fictitious character)—Juvenile literature. 4. Science fiction—Authorship—Juvenile literature.
  [1. Shelley, Mary Wollstonecraft, 1797–1851. 2. Authors, English. 3. Women—Biography.] I. Title. II. Series: Barnard biography series (Berkeley, Calif.)
PR5398.N47   1998
823'.7—dc21
[b]   98–27023
                                                                        CIP
                                                                        AC

Printed in the United States of America on recycled paper.

10 9 8 7 6 5 4 3 2 1

Contents

Acknowledgments

To my agent, Barbara Kouts, for her alertness in finding a publisher.

To the class in Advanced Non-Fiction Techniques at The Writer's Voice of New York's West Side Y, for a close and careful critique of an early chapter.

To the Wertheimer Study of the New York Public Library, for research space.

To Anne Bernays and Justin Kaplan, for their advice and encouragement at a time when both were sorely needed.

To Catherine Gourley, my first editor at Conari Press, for her superb critique of the first five chapters, her understanding, and her infinite patience.

To Claudia Schaab, my present editor, for her intelligent comments and painstaking attention to detail.

To Carol Howard and Ross Hamilton, for their illuminating comments.

To Joe Kane, for his expertise and excellent video library.

To Catherine Nichols and Brian Boucher, for nagging me to get this done.

Foreword

FRANKENSTEIN'S MOTHER

Along with "Scrooge," "Uriah Heep," "Romeo," "Don Juan," "Casper Milquetoast," and a very few others, "Frankenstein" has been transformed from a fictional name to a noun identified with a particular human trait. I can't imagine a compliment more gratifying to a writer of fiction than this, for it means that your character is too real to be confined within the pages of a book.

It doesn't seem to matter that Frankenstein is not the monster's name but that of his creator, a young man whose first name is Victor and who finds himself driven to find "the philosopher's stone and the elixir of life." Over the 180 years since *Frankenstein,* the novel, was published, the monster and the man who brought him to life have melted into one another.

The creator of this creator was Mary Shelley, born in London in 1797; she was only nineteen when she wrote *Frankenstein.* In this book, the story of Mary Shelley's sad life, we're told that *Frankenstein* is the first science fiction novel, even though it has often been mis-identified as merely another "gothic" novel. Scientists had recently discovered a good deal about the nature of electricity; in 1791 a scientist named Luigi Galvani discovered that he could make the muscles of a dead frog twitch by applying electric current to them. The possibilities suggested by this simple experiment seemed mind-boggling. Why not zap any form of inert matter with electricity and bring it to life? The imagination of Mary Shelley, the daughter of remarkably creative parents, Mary Wollstonecraft and William Godwin, was sparked into action by this notion of bringing life from the lifeless. The fact is, Mary Shelley did just that, by inventing a timeless—and poignant— monster.

Mary had a very hard time of it; her life was punctuated by one terrible disappointment after another. To begin with, her mother, the redoubtable Mary Wollstonecraft, a radical and author of *A Vindication of the Rights of Woman,* died four days after giving birth to Mary. Her father, William Godwin, also a radical author, remarried a woman whom Mary didn't care for (Mary thought of her as an "odious woman") and who didn't especially like Mary either. Family life was difficult in spite of Godwin's deep affection for his daughter. Like most writers, Mary had an imagination that thrived on reading—which she did in great gulps, mainly adventure stories and fairy-tales. She often paid long visits to her mother's grave in London; the first words she learned to read were those that made up her mother's name on her gravestone.

Poet Percy Bysshe Shelley, a radical, an atheist, and a married man—though separated from his wife, Harriet, by whom he had a daughter—was a disciple of Mary's father and a frequent visitor to the Godwin establishment. There the twenty-one-year-old poet fell in love with sixteen-year-old Mary; his affection was returned.

Both raging romantics, nourished on melodramatic fiction and gothic tales of the supernatural, Mary and Percy were what used to be called "soulmates." In those days a single woman who was found to have engaged in sex with any man, let alone someone else's husband, was a disgrace shunned by polite society. William Godwin came down hard on his daughter and demanded that she stop seeing Shelley. Love won out over prudence and the pair eloped (without getting married) to Switzerland.

In exile, the young couple met and became friends with England's premier poet, the libertine Lord Byron, and soon they were neighbors on the shore of Lake Leman, near Geneva in Switzerland. One night at a small party, Byron suggested each one write a "ghost story." This was all Mary needed as a trigger.

Over the weeks a frightening story took shape inside her head, focusing on what would happen were a lifeless body revived. Joan Nichols has got it exactly right: "Like Mary's hero, Victor Frankenstein, the young scientist who cobbled his monster together out of parts of dead bodies, a novelist gathers pieces from here and there, arranges them into a definite shape, then uses her genius to spark them into life." All the more amazing in that she was still under twenty and had never before written a novel. Into her story Mary wove, both consciously and—we must assume—unconsciously, the travails of her life and that of her family, as well as the wounds she suffered at the hands of the two men she loved most—her father and Shelley, whom she finally married in 1816. As for the name Victor, this was what Shelley had called himself as a boy. For all his sensitivity as a poet, Percy Shelley was often thoughtless, selfish, and even cruel. Mary, who loved him nevertheless, was convinced that only when people take responsibility for their behavior are they worthy human beings. Much as she loved Shelley, she was painfully aware of his shortcomings as a mate. Thus, the final blame for the monster's evil behavior lies with his creator, Victor, who refuses from the start to assume the role of moral guide for his "child."

One of the most striking features of *Frankenstein* is that its author, still a teenager, was able to get deep inside her main characters and to empathize with both the wretched monster and its equally wretched architect. Here's the monster talking: "I was, besides, endued with a figure hideously deformed and loathsome; I was not even of the same nature as man. . . . Was I then . . . a blot upon the earth, from which all men fled, and whom all men disowned? I cannot describe to you the agony that these reflections inflicted upon me. . . ." And here's Victor Frankenstein, mining much the same emotional vein: "Alas! I had turned loose into the world a depraved wretch, whose delight was in carnage and misery; had he not murdered my brother? No one can conceive the anguish I suffered during the remainder of the night. . . ." Mary Shelley has made the reader experience the heartache of both the man and his monster—not an easy thing to accomplish, especially when her principal tool is what our modern ears would deem a decidedly overheated prose style.

When Percy Shelley drowned in a storm off the Italian coast, Mary was left a widow. She was all of twenty-five. She had given birth four times; only one child lived past babyhood; death during childhood was far more common in the nineteenth century that it is today, but when you think that the first half of Mary's life—she died in England at the age of fifty-three—was punctuated by the death of three children and a husband, it's a wonder she could gather herself together sufficiently to devote the last half to her own fiction and nonfiction and to edit and promote her husband's work.

The temptation, when writing about a conspicuously creative woman, is to put a feminist spin on her life's story. I'm going to avoid this because I don't think it's productive to place a twentieth-century grid over a nineteenth-century life, a period when almost every one of society's conventions and expectations was totally different from those of today. I can only ask the reader to consider carefully a work of fiction in which the dominating figure is a male variously described as "demon," "animal," "monster," "wretch," "devil," "ogre," "fiend," and "vile insect."

—Anne Bernays

Anne Bernays is the author of eight novels, among them the award-winning *Growing Up Rich* and *Professor Romeo*. She has also published numerous short stories, poems, essays, travel pieces, and book reviews. Her most recent book, coauthored with her husband Justin Kaplan, is *The Language of Names*. She has taught fiction writing since 1975, is a cofounder of PEN/New England, and is on the Advisory Board of the National Writers Union. Born in New York City in 1930, she has three daughters, five grandsons, and one granddaughter.

The question so very frequently asked of me—how I, then a young girl, came to think of and to dilate upon so very hideous an idea. . . .

—from the Introduction to *Frankenstein*
by Mary Shelley

ONE

Frankenstein's Mother

> I slept, indeed, but I was disturbed by the wildest
> dreams. . . . I thought that I held the corpse of my
> dead mother in my arms; a shroud enveloped her
> form, and I saw the grave-worms crawling in the
> folds of the flannel.
>
> —from *Frankenstein* by Mary Shelley

A dreadful creature, still reeking of the graveyard parts
from which he was assembled, opens his dull yellow
eyes and breathes. Cowering before him is a pale-faced
young scientist, horror-struck by what he has brought to
life. In that moment Dr. Victor Frankenstein became the
father of a monster who has haunted the world's imagination ever since.

The true mother of Frankenstein and his monster,
however, was Mary Wollstonecraft Godwin Shelley, who
conceived them both when she was nineteen years old.

Even as a young girl, Mary had a taste for graveyards.
Her slender figure in its loose muslin dress and flat-heeled

shoes could often be seen threading its way through the streets of early nineteenth-century London toward old St. Pancras churchyard, the site of her mother's grave.

It was a long walk to the outskirts of the city, but Mary didn't mind. In her early teens, pale and pretty with delicate features and almond-shaped eyes that changed from gray to hazel under a cloud of light reddish-brown hair, she looked more fragile than she was. Besides, no matter how long the walk, it was worth it to get away from her large, mismatched (five children, no two parents in common), and often irritating family.

Leaving behind the schoolroom she shared with her half-sister Fanny and her stepsister Jane, and the sound of young William's boots thumping and clattering through the rickety five-story house, Mary pattered down the stump-a-stump staircase, past the study where her father spent his days writing and receiving callers under the watchful eyes of the portrait of his first wife. Down another flight of stairs and she was in the bookshop. She slipped past her stepmother, busy with customers, and emerged from under the carved figure of Aesop that hung above the door of M. J. Godwin & Co. Displayed in the corner shop's curved window were the children's books her father and stepmother published and sold.

She walked west along Skinner Street, past milliners, furriers, coffee dealers, oil shops, and warehouses. Like most streets in nineteenth-century London, Skinner Street was noisy with the clatter of horses' hooves and iron-wheeled carts careening over cobblestones, smelly and dirty with the contents of chamber pots flung from upper windows and running through the open sewers of

2

the streets, cruel with rowdies like the gangs around the corner on Snow Hill who were known to shove old women into barrels and roll them downhill.

A few blocks to the northeast, live cattle jostled down St. John's Street to Smithfield Market every morning to be sold and slaughtered. One block to the southeast, near Newgate Prison, huge crowds gathered outside the Old Bailey courthouse on hanging days to watch the fun before adjourning to the Magpie and Stump for a pint of ale. Turning her back on these killing fields, Mary continued west along Holborn and then north.

The crowded, dirty, noisy, smelly life of the streets buzzed around her. Playbills plastered shop windows, drunks reeled from beer pubs and gin palaces, peddlers cried their wares, shouts rose from back-alley dogfights and cockfights, ballad singers bawled the story of the latest sensational crime, and eager customers bought cheap broadsheets filled with tales of murder and doomed criminals' last confessions.

As she reached the neighborhood of St. Pancras, the noise and filth fell away. Here, within sight of the green fields of Camden Town, Mary was born and had lived until she was ten years old. Reaching the old church and the peaceful tree-shaded churchyard beside it, she settled down, as always, on her favorite bench next to her mother's tomb.

It was here she came to daydream, to make up stories that would ward off the loneliness she often felt despite her large family and her friends. Something was missing in her life—some beloved companion with whom she could share her innermost hopes and dreams. "Loneliness has been the curse of my life," she later wrote. "What should I have done if my imagination had not been my companion? I must have groveled on the earth—I must have died—O but my dreams my darling sun bright dreams! They peopled the churchyard I was doomed so young to wander in."

Graveyards could be pleasant places in those days; people often treated them like parks, quiet spots of shade and green away from the glare and noise of the city. At night, lovers met and made love among the gravestones. But Mary knew what lay beneath the earth. In some parts of London, burial grounds were so full that from time to time corpses piled on top of each other would break through the surface, emitting a poisonous stench.

At night in St. Sepulchre's churchyard, a few blocks from where Mary lived, grave robbers dug bodies from fresh graves, then sold their gruesome harvest to the surgeons at nearby St. Bartholemew's Hospital, who had few legal ways to get the bodies they needed to dissect and study except from these "resurrection men." Most of the time, Mary was able to keep the two realities separate— the pleasant trees and grass, the old stone church aboveground, the rotting bodies, including her mother's, below.

Mary had been coming to her mother's grave ever since she was a little girl, her hand clasped in her father's. She always recognized it by the two weeping willow trees her father had planted on either side. Sometimes he would take her finger and help her trace the letters carved on the stone: *Mary Wollstonecraft Godwin,* she would repeat after him, her tongue stumbling over the hard words as her finger followed the sharp edges of the stone. *Author of A Vindication of the Rights of Woman, Born 27th April 1759/Died 10th September 1797.* They were the first words she learned to read. Mary Wollstonecraft Godwin was *her* name too, the same name as belonged to the woman who had died giving her daughter life. She'd heard the story many times.

During the summer of 1797, immense storms had ravaged England. Tidal floods and whirling waterspouts struck the coast. Floods lay waste large parts of the country. Frightening electrical storms rife with fireballs and lightning ripped across the skies. A freak hailstorm killed birds by the score.

At No. 29, the Polygon, one of a ring of connected houses on the outskirts of London, Mary Wollstonecraft Godwin, the famous author of *A Vindication of the Rights of Woman,* awaited the birth of her second child. As the rains beat down on the fields of Somers Town, lashed the windows, roared about the roof, she worked on her latest novel, *Maria, or the Wrongs of Woman.* Throughout the day, she sent and received notes from her husband, William Godwin, like herself a famous radical writer, where he worked in his rooms at No. 17, Evesham Buildings, some twenty doors away. And she looked after her little daughter, three-year-old Fanny, who loved to romp with her adored mama, especially on the mornings she stayed in her room and breakfasted in bed.

On August 14, the weather calmed. Amazed Londoners saw a circle of glowing light appear in the night sky. For eleven days, the unexpected comet shone above the city. Mary and William Godwin called it their unborn baby's lucky star.

Mary wasn't one to make a fuss about the difficulties of childbirth. She looked forward to her upcoming delivery without fear. Despite her age, she was in good health and had delivered Fanny easily. She would have the baby at home, she decided, attended by a midwife. Midwives and male doctors had fought for control of childbirth for more than a century: Doctors claimed that midwives were ignorant; midwives said that doctors were jargon-spouting quacks too quick to use instruments. Mary Wollstonecraft, mother of feminism, had faith in her own sex. On Wednesday, August 30, when she went into labor, she called in Mrs. Blenkinsop, matron and midwife to the Westminster Lying-In Hospital.

Mary's attitude was lighthearted but impatient. "I have no doubt of seeing the animal today," she wrote Godwin. "Pray send me the newspaper. I wish I had a novel or some book of sheer amusement to excite curiosity and while away the time."

And later, "Mrs. Blenkinsop tells me I am in the most natural state, and can promise me a safe delivery, but that I must have a little patience."

Eight hours later, her patience was rewarded. Just before midnight, a healthy baby girl was born. Godwin recorded the event in his diary: "Birth of Mary, 20 minutes after 11 at night."

Although the birth was normal, the placenta, usually expelled a few minutes after birth, failed to appear. Dr. Poignard, a physician at the Westminster Hospital, came to remove it by hand—a long, painful, bloody process. It was 8 A.M. before he was done. Mary was weak but otherwise had come through her ordeal in fine shape. Her friend, Dr. Fordyce, also a believer in midwives, stopped in to see her. Later that day, he told a friend, "Mary had had a woman, and was doing extremely well."

But despite appearances, she was not doing well. And it wasn't Mrs. Blenkinsop who was to blame. Doctors at the time, knowing nothing of the causes of infection, didn't sterilize their hands or their instruments. During the long hours Dr. Poignard had spent removing the placenta, he had introduced infection into Mary's body. In attempting to save her life, he had unknowingly caused her death.

For the next two days, however, Mary seemed fine. She gained strength; friends came to visit. She and Godwin cooed over the new baby. But on Saturday evening, she felt ill and woke on Sunday with violent shivering fits. Septicemia, or blood poisoning, had set in. This serious, even fatal, condition is caused by harmful bacteria entering the bloodstream, often after a surgical procedure. The bacteria multiply and invade other organs, causing fever, chills, and sweating and infecting the lungs, kidneys, and brain. Antibiotics would have cured it, but in 1797 they didn't exist.

Doctors came and went, but Mary only grew worse. Fanny and the new baby were sent to a friend's house. Godwin sat by his wife's bedside, offering her sips of wine to take the edge off her pain. By Thursday, it was clear that she was dying. During the next two days, husband and wife talked quietly of her death and of the children she was leaving behind. Her last words were of her husband: "He is the kindest, best man in the world."

On Sunday morning, September 10, Mary Wollstonecraft died. Godwin, who recorded everything in his diary, wrote only "20 minutes before 8" followed by three blank lines. He was too grief-stricken to attend her funeral. On Friday, she was buried in St. Pancras churchyard in the company of a few close friends.

Her daughter Mary, eleven days old when her mother died, had begun her life shadowed by death, a shadow that would loom again and again. A major theme of Mary Shelley's life story is the death of those she most loved. Perhaps it's not surprising that she grew up to create a hero who snatched dead bodies from the grave and made them live.

TWO

Nobody's Girl but Papa's

And thou, strange star! ascendant at my birth
Which rained, they said, kind influence on the earth
So from great parents sprung, I dared boast
Fortune my friend. . . .

—from *The Choice* by Mary Shelley

The little fair-haired girl, only two and a half years old, strained and stretched to see across the fields to the trees at Camden Town. Papa was gone. He'd been away for days and days, and though Mary had watched across the fields she hadn't seen him come striding up. Papa hadn't left her alone, of course. She had Fanny, her big sister, for company, and as always Mrs. Jones looked after her; other nice ladies, friends of Papa's, also came and made a fuss. And when Papa left, he invited his friend Mr. Marshall, who was a very nice man, to come and stay. But Papa had been away so long. What if he was never coming back? Perhaps he had given her to Mr. Marshall to be his little girl. She was very much afraid.

Now Mr. Marshall said he had a letter from Papa and in it was a message for Mary. Papa hadn't forgotten her. Somehow he knew what she had feared. Mr. Marshall read aloud the comforting words: "Tell Mary, I will not give her away, and she shall be nobody's little girl but Papa's. Papa is gone away, but Papa will very soon come back again, and see the Polygon across two fields from the trunks of the trees at Camden Town."

Mary adored her father. Her love for him was the earliest feeling she could remember. Until she was sixteen, she said, "I may justly say that he was my God." As a little girl, being allowed to leave her nurse to be with Papa filled her with pride. She'd sit and stare at him, waiting for the look or gesture that said she could come near. He was the fixed point in her life, the one she could rely on. When she was naughty, all he had to do was look at her with silent disapproval, and she would cry.

Her father's fixed point, however, was gone. William Godwin had grieved for months after his wife's death. Nowhere, he told a friend, was there a woman who had combined such a clear and deep intelligence "with so much goodness of heart and sweetness of manners" as his late wife. Her equal didn't exist. He would never get over his loss. "I have not the least expectation that I can now ever know happiness again."

He turned her bedroom into his study. Here he devoted himself to editing her works and writing her life story, *Memoirs of the Author of* A Vindication of the Rights of Woman. He hung her portrait, painted a few months before she died, where he could see it as he worked. Every day when Mary visited him, she saw her mother's serene and beautiful face gazing dreamily into the distance. A portrait of her father hung facing it across the room, just as her parents might have faced each other across a table, if her mother were still alive.

Mary Wollstonecraft had cut a wide swath through her times, scandalizing people right and left, even her radical friends. In a time when most women were raised to be husband catchers, she had struggled to earn her own living and make a name for herself. She had felt the wrongs done to women on her own skin. In 1792, when she was in her early thirties, she wrote *A Vindication of the Rights of Woman,* a fervent defense of women's equality. It brought instant fame and guaranteed her immortality. She was a woman of great mind and great heart; when she gave, she gave all and was shocked and dismayed when her generosity wasn't returned. Independent and intellectual, witty and warm, tender yet passionate, Mary Wollstonecraft Godwin was a hard act to follow.

She had been part of a circle of English freethinkers who sympathized with the aims and spirit of the French Revolution. When an angry mob stormed the Bastille prison on July 14, 1789, she had been thrilled and inspired. Fierce for the rights of man and *woman,* she'd sped across the English Channel to Paris to get a look at events for herself. There she'd fallen in love with an American adventurer, Gilbert Imlay, the great passion of her life, and bore his child, her daughter Fanny.

Her passionate nature and generosity of spirit served her poorly in dealing with Imlay, who never regarded their affair as seriously as she did. When he took another mistress, she fell into despair and tried to kill herself, not once, but twice.

By the mid-1790s, the ideals of the French Revolution

had disintegrated into the blood and gore of the Reign of Terror. Mary Wollstonecraft heard the rumbles of the cart carrying King Louis XVI to the guillotine. Soon hundreds of men and women were having their heads chopped off every week. France had decided to carry its revolution to the rest of Europe. By 1793, it was at war with many countries, including Great Britain.

In 1794, Mary returned to an England full of frightened middle- and upper-class people, sure their own lower classes were about to turn on them. Newspapers were full of rumors of bloodthirsty revolutionaries out to destroy society. Cartoonists drew huge guillotines dripping with blood. Because of the war, prices rose. Poor people couldn't get food to eat. As King George III drove through the streets, a crowd of perhaps 200,000 pressed against his coach, shouting, "No king! Give us peace and bread."

For the first time, the British government set agents to spy on its own people. Censorship increased. The "Gagging Acts" of November 1795 restricted public meetings and speechmaking. Anyone who favored progressive or radical ideas was identified with the "republican, regicidal, atheistic French."

Mary Wollstonecraft, now a struggling single mother, needed a rest from passion and politics. In 1796, she met and fell in love with William Godwin, a man as kind, intelligent, and humorous as herself. He was a thinker, not a doer. "I am bold and adventurous in opinions, not in life," he said of himself quite accurately. He was almost forty when he met Mary and had his first love affair.

Godwin's fame rested on his book *Political Justice* as

hers did on *A Vindication of the Rights of Woman*. Get rid of all institutions, he wrote, from the government to the family. Share the wealth. Make reason the supreme guide. Keep emotions in check. Realizing that our greatest happiness is the happiness of all, practice "universal benevolence"; individuals should be happy to sacrifice themselves, he thought, if society in general benefited.

He had published his book in 1793 to wide acclaim. Writer William Hazlitt said, "No one was more talked of, more looked up to, more sought after, and wherever liberty, truth, justice was the theme, his name was not far off." Now, just a few years later, Godwin and his book seemed deeply subversive. In the new conservative climate, both were ridiculed and reviled.

Neither Godwin nor Wollstonecraft believed in marriage—"a monopoly, and the worst of monopolies," Godwin called it. They agreed to live in neighboring houses, write daily notes to each other, and visit by appointment. Then Mary became pregnant. An affair was one thing, single motherhood something else entirely. Mary hated the thought of the scandal, the pointing fingers, the shame of illegitimacy thrust upon her child. She was also mortified, afraid that Godwin might see her pregnancy as a burden she was placing on him. She pushed him away. "I can abide by the consequence of my own conduct," she told him, "and do not wish to involve anyone in my difficulties."

But he loved her. Of course he'd marry her, for her sake and the child's. The *London Times* wedding announcement poked sly fun: "Mr. Godwin, author of a Pamphlet against the Institution of Marriage, to the famous Mrs.

Wollstonecraft, who wrote in support of the *Rights of Woman.*"

They moved into one of a ring of thirty-two attached houses on the outskirts of London, called, collectively, the Polygon. Theirs was No. 29. Godwin also took rooms in nearby Chalton Street, where he could work and sometimes sleep. The Godwins had bowed to convention by marrying, but still did not intend to live in each other's pockets. "A husband is a convenient part of the furniture of a house," Mary wrote, "unless he be a clumsy fixture. I wish you, from my soul, to be riveted in my heart; but I do not desire to have you always at my elbow."

Now she was gone from his elbow, gone from his life. The increased social sympathy and respectability Mary Wollstonecraft had gained by marrying disappeared after her death when Godwin published his *Memoirs of the Author of* A Vindication of the Rights of Woman. He left no secrets untold. Because he had loved her for her courage, her daring, her passionate nature, so unlike his own, he assumed that everyone else would feel the same. He seems to have been unaware of how the world would regard her affair with Imlay, her two suicide attempts, and her illegitimate child. In sexual matters as in politics, public attitudes had shifted during the 1790s. The close-knit family was the ideal. Talk of woman's independence and sexual freedom was taboo.

With his wife dead, Godwin felt overwhelmed by new responsibilities. "The poor children! I am totally unfitted to educate them," he wrote. "I am the most unfit person for this office; she was the best qualified in the world. What a change."

From the first, Godwin had resolved to treat both girls equally, even though only one was his. He didn't plan to tell Fanny that she was the daughter of Gilbert Imlay, her mother's former lover, until he thought she was old enough to understand. Godwin was always warm and loving to Fanny. She bore his name, and he treated her like his own daughter.

If he was partial to his daughter Mary and had a greater interest in her future, that was only natural. After all, she was the child of not one, but two remarkable parents. Did she, he wondered, show signs of inherited genius? Godwin believed in physiognomy, the art of studying the features of a person's face to discern character and intelligence. When Mary was three weeks old, he called in an expert named Mr. Nicholson to examine her.

Mr. Nicholson did the best he could with the wriggling infant thrust into his arms. Her mouth might promise intelligence, he told her anxious father, although, because she wouldn't keep it still it was hard to be sure. He also saw signs of a good memory, sensibility, and affection. Impatience too, but not violent anger. "She was displeased, and it denoted much more of resigned vexation than either scorn or rage."

A devoted nursemaid named Cooper cared for the girls' physical needs. For mothering, they had a friend of Godwin's sister, Louisa Jones, who took over as housekeeper. A warm, loving person, honored to be in charge of the daughters of Mary Wollstonecraft, she did her best to follow Wollstonecraft's theories of child care. Luckily for the girls, this meant light, loose clothing, lots of hugging and playing, and plenty of exercise and fresh air.

Fanny, who remembered her mother, resented Louisa. But baby Mary loved her; she was the closest thing to a real mother she ever had.

Then, suddenly, when Mary was fifteen months old, Louisa left in a flurry of tears. She had perhaps hoped to become the girls' stepmother, but that was not to be. Aunts and family friends stepped in to share the motherly role. Later, Louisa took to dropping in a few days each week to look after the girls but was no longer a regular part of the household.

Despite the lack of a mother, Mary was happy during her first few years of life. She had a daily routine she could count on, a big sister to keep her company, family and friends to dote on her, and the freedom to run and play and be as close to nature as her mother would have wished.

The children's nursery was on the third floor, their father's study below them, the servants' rooms in the attic above. A balcony faced the street. Each house had its own little walled garden. As soon as she was old enough, Mary helped Fanny and Mr. Collins, the gardener, make sure its crop of strawberries and beans was kept "spruce, cropped, weeded, and mowed." In the country fields and meadows that stretched around the house, she and Fanny were allowed to run wild at a time when most little girls were not.

In the mornings, though, Mary and Fanny were told to play quietly in the nursery while Papa worked. At one o'clock, when Papa rang his bell for lunch, they could visit him for half an hour. Then, if it was a fine day, he took them for a walk across the fields. When they returned, there would be guests come to see Papa—important people who talked and talked, young men who listened when Papa spoke, hanging on his words. Fanny and Mary would be called in to meet them. Mary liked the young men who joked and played with her and called her "little sister Mary."

Papa's older friends visited too, many of them famous though Mary didn't care about that. The essayist Charles Lamb, as merry as a child himself, came often with his sister, Mary. So did Samuel Taylor Coleridge, the famous poet, who called Mary "a fat little creature." To his wife, Sara, she was "dear meek little Mary." Their son Hartley had a crush on Mary when he was three and a half and she a year younger. Once, when he knew his father was writing Godwin a letter, he told him to send Mary his love.

"What? and not to Fanny?" his father protested.

"Yes, and to Fanny, but I'll *have* Mary," Hartley said.

Sometimes there were trips into the heart of London to pay visits and see the circus and musical plays and wild animals at the menagerie. When a hot-air balloonist made the first parachute jump in England into a nearby field, the Godwins went to watch.

Mary saw her Grandma Godwin, who lived in the country, less often. She was an energetic, gossipy woman, not well educated, but devoted to her family. Letters from her, full of eccentric spelling, outspoken opinions, and common sense, arrived regularly along with gifts—"a new piece of print for my grand-daughter Mary for a gown with 2/6 to pay for the making, a pr. little Stokens [stockings] and Hat."

When Mary was three, her grandmother sent her a box, probably of silver, used for holding snuff, a kind of pulverized tobacco. "I did not mean the snuffbox for a plaything for Mary," Mrs. Godwin admonished her son. "It is of value, but for you to take care of till she knows its value, and is told it was her grandfather's present to her grandmother."

As a Dissenter, a Protestant nonconformist in the Puritan tradition, Mrs. Godwin held strict views on conduct. Godwin, who had grown away from the beliefs on which he'd been reared, was a freethinker who believed in neither God nor marriage. Despite their extreme differences of belief, Mrs. Godwin didn't let the radical ideas of her famous, forty-year-old son keep her from loving him. Nor did she hesitate to sometimes say, "I told you so." In 1798, when she received a copy of the *Memoirs,* she wasn't shocked by the frank account of Mary Wollstonecraft's love affairs and suicide attempts, but she was quick to point out a lesson:

> I hope you are taught by reflection your mistake concerning marriage. There might have been two children that had no lawful right to anything that was their father's, with a thousand other bad consequences, children and wives crying about the streets without a protector. You wish, I dare say, to keep your own opinion, therefore I shall say no more but wish you and the dear babes happy. Does little Mary thrive? or she weaned? You will follow your wife's direction, give them a good deal of air, and have a good opportunity, as you live out of the smoke of the city.

(Mrs. Godwin may not have approved of her late daughter-in-law's morals, but did agree with her on the subject of fresh air!)

As the worst of his grief subsided, Godwin's own feelings were of emptiness. Though he'd returned to his bachelor routine of writing in the morning and visiting friends at night, life wasn't the same. He'd acquired a taste for marriage. Besides, he worried about bringing up two motherless girls on his own. He proposed in turn to two intelligent, well-educated women, friends of his who would have made good stepmothers for his little girls. Unfortunately, both turned him down.

Then, when Mary was three years old, a family moved in next door to No. 27, the Polygon—a mother and two children. One day, Godwin was sitting on his balcony, his books and papers spread out around him; it was a pleasant place to write. Engrossed in his work, he may not even have seen the woman who stepped out from her house onto the balcony next door. But she saw him. Leaning over, she waved and trilled, "Is it possible that I behold the immortal Godwin?"

He was flattered. He was lonely. Mrs. Clairmont, as she called herself, was interested and available and right next door. Although she passed as a widow, she had never married; her children had different fathers. That, of course, would not have mattered to a freethinker like Godwin. Besides, she was plump and pretty with curly blonde hair.

Soon both families were friendly and going about together on little jaunts. In no time at all, by the end of December 1801, Godwin and Mary Jane Clairmont were married.

Suddenly, the house at No. 29 bulged with people. Mary, now four years old, and Fanny had to share the nursery with a new brother and sister—Charles, who became the older brother Mary had never had, and Jane, one year younger, destined to be her friend—and foe—for the rest of her life.

Mary's life in a childhood Garden of Eden had ended. With a stepmother to contend with, she was no longer "nobody's girl but Papa's." With so many new rivals for his love and attention, how could she keep her special place in Papa's heart?

THREE

Cinderella

Next day to view a vast balloon
    The folks came far and near,
To see it start John hurried soon,
    For ev'ry sight was dear.

He ask'd a woman on the ground
    Who paid for the balloon,
But "Je vous n'entends pas" he found
    Was still the only tune.

Says he, "I now don't wonder, Dame,
    "To find 'tis his balloon,
"For sure the Nongtonpaw can claim
    "All that's beneath the moon."

> —from "Mounseer Nongtongpaw"
> by Mary Godwin, age ten

Mary Jane Clairmont, the new Mrs. Godwin, was no Mary Wollstonecraft. She had neither her brains, talent, looks, character, nor charm, and she knew it. She drove away most of the people young Mary loved best with her bad temper, lies, sullenness, and envy: Mary's nurse, Cooper; Mr. Marshall; her substitute mothers—friends, aunts, and above all, Louisa Jones.

Godwin's old friends didn't like Mary Jane, and she didn't like them. Charles Lamb and his sister called her the "Bad Baby" because of her temper and sullen pouts. They said she was like the spiteful sister in the fairytale "Toads and Diamonds," who spewed slimy toads when she spoke. In fact, Lamb went so far as to call her "a damn'd infernal bitch."

Godwin wasn't blind to his wife's faults. While they were still courting, he'd written her notes on how to correct them: "My dear love, take care of yourself. Manage and economize your temper. It is at bottom most excellent: do not let it be soured and spoiled." Unpleasant traits she'd more or less managed to suppress when courting appeared in force once she was married.

Mrs. G., Mary's private name for her, made no secret of favoring her own children, Charles and Jane and young William, born on March 28, 1803, when Mary was five and a half. But she resented Mary's closeness to Godwin. Although Mary tried to keep her feelings hidden, her stepmother quickly discovered what Mary later described as, "my excessive and romantic attachment to my father."

Despite Mrs. G.'s temper and the creaks and strains involved in blending two families into one, the household was easygoing. Like other middle-class people of his time, Godwin had no intention of bringing up his children as strictly as he'd been brought up, even though Grandma Godwin never stopped hoping her son would give up atheism and return to "spiritual things, and instruct your dear children in the same. It's a duty incumbent on parents. We may see every day [children's] proneness to evil and backwardness to that which is good. You cannot be insensible of that. I cannot write otherwise, so you must not be offended."

Godwin wasn't offended, but he didn't agree. This was a new time. Gone were autocratic fathers and formal manners, the custom of farming infants out to wet nurses, and the insistence on beatings to break a child's will. Although other people might look after children's day-to-day needs, parents saw their children often and gave them their full attention when they did. It was the Victorians later in the nineteenth century who brought strictness and formality back into family life. The family Mary Godwin grew up in, like most families today, valued companionship, equality, and individual rights.

Godwin prided himself on being a good father. Someone once accused him of championing infanticide. He was incensed. Wasn't he a lover of children? Wasn't his own household run solely for the benefit of his children? "Are not my children my favourite companions and most chosen friends?"

And yet he could be stern. Although he liked to see and cultivate his children's growing independence, he had no patience with disobedience, anger, or jealousy. Feelings they might have, but feelings were to be kept under control.

Although Godwin prided himself on his ability to be fair and objective, Mary was clearly his favorite child.

People were always curious to know how the daughters of the famous Mary Wollstonecraft were turning out. To one inquirer he wrote:

> . . . my own daughter is considerably superior in capacity to the one her mother had before. Fanny, the eldest, is of a quiet, modest, unshowy disposition, somewhat given to indolence, which is her greatest fault, but sober, observing, peculiarly clear and distinct in the faculty of memory, and disposed to exercise her own thoughts and follow her own judgment.

Mary, on the other hand, was

> singularly bold, somewhat imperious, and active of mind. Her desire of knowledge is great, and her perseverance in everything she undertakes is almost invincible. [She] is, I believe, very pretty.

The best way for Mary to keep her place in her father's heart was to be what he wanted her to be—the inheritor of her mother's genius. For that she needed to be educated. But how was a girl to be taught and what should she learn?

For old-fashioned people like Mary's grandmother, the answer was simple: religion and needlework, taught at home. Grandma Godwin sent five-year-old Mary a Bible and her hopes that her son would "promote the knowledge of the undoubted truths in it." A few months later, she wrote, "I would advise you to let your children learn to knit little worsted short stockings, just above their shoes, to keep their feet from chilblains this winter."

Fashionable, up-to-date people thought girls should learn "accomplishments," such as French, singing, painting in watercolors, and fancy needlework, to help them catch a husband and to stay busy until they did. In *A Vindication of the Rights of Woman,* Wollstonecraft had heaped scorn on this "false system." Developing as a human being, she insisted, was more important than pleasing men. Raise girls like boys to exercise their minds and bodies and train for careers.

Oh no, argued Maria Edgeworth, a popular writer of books for children and adults, in *Practical Education.* Girls must adapt to the world as it is, not as it might be. Have them learn caution, restraint, and dignity, not spiritedness. Teach them to accept "the impossibility of their rambling about the world in quest of adventures."

How were the daughters of Mary Wollstonecraft being educated? an acquaintance asked. Godwin admitted that, "The present Mrs. Godwin has great strength and activity in mind, but is not exclusively a follower of the notions of their mother." Nor did he have time to put "novel theories of education to practice."

The present Mrs. Godwin believed that each child should be educated to some definite duties and with a view toward filling some useful place in the world. In Mary's view, household drudgery was the life work her stepmother saw for her and Fanny; all the money the family could spare and more should go to educate Jane and let her acquire accomplishments. The two boys, Charles and William, were sent to a nearby day school. The three girls were taught at home by a capable governess, Miss Maria Smith; needlework was included among her subjects. Both boys and girls had their share of chores. They ate simple food to nourish their bodies and slept on hard beds. "Plain living and high thinking are no more," complained poet William Wordsworth. Clearly his friend Coleridge hadn't told him about life at the Godwin home.

In fact, Mary received an excellent education. Being among Godwin's circle of friends was an education in itself. One evening Samuel Taylor Coleridge came to recite his long narrative poem, *The Rime of the Ancient Mariner.* Mary and Jane hid under the sofa to listen.

> It is an ancient Mariner,
> And he stoppeth one of three.
> "By thy long gray beard and glittering eye,
> Now wherefore stopps't thou me?"

Mary was at once caught up in the grim world of the doomed outcast, forced to roam the world relating the story of his sin and its eerie consequences. Then she or Jane moved, or sniffled, or sneezed, and they were discovered, dragged out, ordered to bed. Coleridge, perhaps flattered, begged Mrs. G. to let them stay. She gave in and so Mary got to hear the whole of a poem that would stick in her mind for years.

Most of all, Mary read—fiction, fairy-tales, adventure stories, anything to foster her imagination. Godwin detested fact books like *A Tour Through Papa's House,* which explained how furniture was made, carpets woven, and "the history and manufacture of iron." A person could happily live and die without ever knowing any of the stuff people tried to force into the heads of children, he said, facts that "freeze up the soul" and give a "premature taste for clearness and exactness." Better to cultivate children's imaginations, which will fire their ambition and teach them empathy.

Luckily, there was plenty of imaginative children's literature to choose from. Between 1750 and 1814, children's book writers, members of a new profession, produced a wide range of some 2,400 books costing between a penny and sixpence each. By the time Mary learned to read (from lessons her mother had written shortly before she died), books for children no longer had to point to a moral. They could be just for fun.

Mary read Mrs. Barbauld's four little books for beginners and *The Infant's Friend* by Mrs. Lovechild, then moved on to the recently published fairy-tales of Charles Perrault—*Little Red Riding Hood, Beauty and the Beast,* and the rest—then on to *Valentine and Orson, Robinson Crusoe,* and *The Arabian Nights.*

When Mary read Perrault's *Cinderella,* the wicked stepmother, favored stepsisters, and poor, put-upon heroine must have struck a familiar chord. Mary had only one troublesome stepsister to contend with, but she was enough. There was no question that dark-haired, dark-eyed, clever Jane, petted and spoiled, was her mother's favorite child.

Jane, on the other hand, was jealous of Mary because she was her father's favorite and because everyone made such a fuss over her famous mother. Whereas Mary was bold and bright and somewhat bossy, Jane, like her mother, pouted and needed to be coaxed back into a good mood. Flareups, fighting, and tears were inevitable. Many years later, as a middle-aged woman, Mary was to say of Jane, with some slight exaggeration, "She has been the bane of my existence since I was two."

But Mary and Jane were also two little girls close in age, each lacking a parent. They couldn't help playing together and being friends. It was an uneasy alliance. Sometimes they were as close as sisters, sometimes they hated each other, also like sisters. Jealous of each other, envious, and complaining, they helped and supported each other, too. The pattern of their relationship that took form in the nursery was to last all their lives.

Mary's dislike of Mrs. Godwin was to last a lifetime, too. For all her faults, the "wicked stepmother" was hardworking and clever. Taking on Godwin's family was a difficult task. It could not have been easy to see the portrait of the first Mrs. Godwin, now almost a saint in her husband's eyes, staring down at her from the walls of his study every day; nor easy when visitors asked Mary to stand beneath it so they could trace her similarity to her mother; nor easy juggling finances, trying to make ends meet.

The family budget was in terrible shape. In the new political climate, Godwin's brand of radicalism had gone out of fashion, and it became harder to sell his books. Unable to earn enough by his writing to support his enlarged family, he was constantly borrowing money from his friends.

Then Mrs. Godwin had an idea. Why not take advantage of the family's interest and knowledge of children and literature and set up a business writing, publishing, and selling children's books? Going into trade was a comedown. Gentlemen were supposed to live off their inherited income or work in the professions, not handle money over a counter. But they were desperate. Godwin borrowed more money from his friends, and in 1805 opened the Juvenile Library of M. J. Godwin and Co. Among the many books it published was Charles and Mary Lamb's *Tales from Shakespeare,* a book popular with children for generations afterward.

At first, home and business were separate. Then in November 1807, when Mary was ten, the family moved away from the fields and trees of Somers Town to a new but rickety five-story building at 41 Skinner Street in Holborn, the dirty heart of the city. The only entrance to their home was through the shop and up the stairs, the creaky floors shaking and trembling with every step. Godwin ensconced himself in a second-floor room shaped like a quadrant—windows in the arc, a fireplace in one radius, a door and shelves crammed with old books in the other—and hung his late wife's portrait on the wall. Here he wrote books for children on history and literature, which Mrs. Godwin sold on the floor below. The girls had the schoolroom and the rest of the third floor to themselves.

Mary and the others were a ready-made audience for Godwin's educational books. The young people would stand in a circle around him and recite the lessons they'd learned from them. Remarkably easy! he claimed they said. They also wrote and memorized essays for Godwin's informal little classes.

It was hardly surprising, as Mary herself noted, that surrounded by books and "as the daughter of two persons of distinguished literary celebrity," she took to writing. "As a child I scribbled, and my favorite pastime during the hours given me for recreation was to 'write stories.'" Yet most of what she wrote was to please other people, "rather doing as others had done than putting down the suggestions of my own mind."

One of these attempts was inspired by a current popular song, "Mounseer Nong Tong Paw," written by a Charles Dibdin for a musical comedy called *The General Election*. Mary adapted and expanded it. Written in verse, "Mounseer Nongtongpaw" tells the story of a comical Englishman, a typical John Bull, who travels in France unable to understand what he hears. Whenever he asks a question, a French person answers, "Je vous n'entends pas," meaning, "I don't understand you." The Englishman, hearing *n'entends pas* as *Nongtongpaw,* thinks it's someone's name and is bowled over by the activities of this strange "mounseer."

Mary showed the result to her father, who sent it on to an acquaintance. Godwin's pride and delight in her accomplishment shine through his deliberately neutral words. "That in small writing," he wrote, "is the production of my daughter in her eleventh year, and is strictly modelled, as far as her infant talent would allow, on Dibdin's song." He had artist William Mulready illustrate Mary's effort. *"Mounseer Nongtongpaw," or, The Discoveries of John Bull in a Trip to Paris,* handsome in its small square shape and brightly colored drawings, came out that month as a child's picture book. Mary Wollstonecraft Godwin, age ten and a half, had become a published author. Her book continued to sell for many years in England and the United States.

Writing and publishing "Mounseer Nongtongpaw" was gratifying, but in Mary's secret heart her imagination took wilder forms. Her dearest pleasure, she said, "was the formation of castles in the air—the indulging in waking dreams—the following up trains of thought, which had for their subject the formation of a succession of imaginary incidents. My dreams were at once more fantastic and agreeable than my writings."

Daydreams were a way to escape Skinner Street and the frustrations and annoyances of family life. More than that, they were the expression of her true self, a secret self she felt she had to keep hidden or risk losing the esteem she enjoyed in her father's eyes.

FOUR

The Mother Tree

They say that thou wert lovely from thy birth,
Of glorious parents, thou aspiring Child.
I wonder not—for One then left this earth
Whose life was like a setting planet mild,
Which clothed thee in the radiance undefiled
Of its departing glory: still her fame
Shines on thee, through the tempests dark and wild
Which shake these latter days. . . .

—from the dedication to *The Revolt of Islam*
by Percy Bysshe Shelley

A s Mary entered her teens, her relationship with the rest of her family grew more and more strained. Her stepmother, an "odious woman" whose name Mary couldn't mention without disgust, had her hands full with a stepdaughter who resisted her at every turn. Jane envied Mary for having the talents Godwin most valued—creativity, imagination, and the ability to write. In their family, Jane claimed, "if you cannot write an epic poem or novel, that by its originality knocks all other novels on the head, you are a despicable creature, not worth acknowledging."

Godwin had grown annoyed with all this friction, especially Mary's inability to get along with her stepmother. When painful pustules—ugly, pimplelike bumps filled with pus—erupted on Mary's hand, her doctor advised six months of saltwater therapy. Sea air was considered a cure for just about anything in the early nineteenth century, so Mrs. Godwin took Mary to Ramsgate on the coast and installed her in a boarding school. "Tell Mary," her father wrote to his wife, "that, in spite of unfavorable appearances, I have still faith that she will become a wise, and, what is more, a good and a happy woman."

Eight months later, in December 1811, Mary returned. She was fourteen years old. Aaron Burr, former vice-president of the United States and a frequent visitor at this time, wrote to his daughter, "Mary has come home, and looks very lovely, but has not the air of strong health." To the friend who introduced him to the family, he added, "There was a pleasure in contemplating the daughter of Mary Wollstonecraft."

Any family can look well on the surface. To Burr and others, the Godwins seemed a happy, industrious, well-educated family, not rich in money, but rich in friends, books, and each other. One evening, to Burr's amusement, young William, then eight years old, mounted a little stand and delivered his regular weekly lecture, just as his father's friends did. Mary had written it for him. "He went through it with great gravity and decorum," Burr noted. "The subject was, 'The influence of governments on the character of a people.' After the lecture we had tea, and the girls sang and danced an hour; and at nine came home."

Burr, a man in his mid-fifties, acted a little silly around the three girls. "Les goddesses," he called Fanny, Mary, and Jane, who were then between thirteen and seventeen years old. He insisted that they all loved him, tried to give them gifts of stockings, and came to see them dressed for a ball—"extremely neat, and with taste."

Despite the balls and lectures, the family parties and famous visitors, Mary's unhappiness grew. The warm, friendly Papa of her childhood seemed to have disappeared. He was too busy, he said, to spend time trying to coax her into good behavior. Instead, he coldly lay down the law and scolded her sternly when she disobeyed. She no longer felt that she could share her thoughts with him. He didn't know who she was. Neither did she.

All children are born strangers into families where everyone else already knows all about one another. Children must piece together this information for themselves over the years of their growing up. Motherless daughters, like Mary, especially seem to need to seek this knowledge, to find out who they are by finding out who their mothers were.

In one version of the *Cinderella* story, Cinderella asks her father to bring her a tree branch from town, which she then plants at her mother's grave. The tree grows and speaks to her in her mother's voice. Just so, Mary Godwin sat beside her mother's grave, hearing her mother's voice in the books she had written and in the memoir her father had written about her, reliving the romantic, free-spirited yet troubled life her mother had led, looking back at a time she never knew, dreaming of her own life that was to come.

To most respectable people, Mary Wollstonecraft's life was a scandal and a shame. But not to her daughter. The more Mary Godwin learned about her mother, the more she idolized her. "Mary Wollstonecraft," she later wrote, "was one of those beings who appear once perhaps in a generation, to gild humanity with a ray which no difference of opinion nor chance of circumstances can cloud. Her genius was undeniable. . . . Many years are passed since that beating heart has been laid in the cold still grave, but no one who has ever seen her speaks of her without enthusiastic veneration."

Consciously or not, Mary modeled herself on the impulsive, reckless side of her mother's nature, as well as on her ideas. What she learned of her mother reinforced what she had already learned from her father: Think for yourself. Share with others. Be strictly honest. Act on your beliefs. Don't whine.

During the six months following Mary's return from Ramsgate, her skin condition grew worse until it affected her whole arm. The doctor prescribed another six months by the sea. A Scottish acquaintance and admirer of Godwin's, William Baxter, offered to have Mary stay at his family home near Dundee, Scotland. The offer came as a relief all around. Godwin jumped at it.

On June 7, 1812, the day came that Mary both yearned for and feared. She was to travel to Scotland on a packet boat, the *Osnaburgh*. Her father took her to the wharf to see her off. Fanny and Jane came too, but not Mrs. G. The four climbed on board. It would be an hour yet before the boat would sail. Mary, who suffered from seasickness, dreaded the voyage itself. And what did she have to look forward to when she arrived? A country she had never seen, a family of people she had never met, and months away from everyone and every place she knew best.

Her father, looking at her, had sudden qualms. She was only fourteen years old, and he was sending her off on a long voyage "with not a single face around her that she had ever seen till that morning." He spoke to the captain. Was there anyone on board to whom he could entrust his daughter? A Mrs. Nelson, of Great St. Helen's, London, was on her way to Scotland to look after her sick husband. Her three grown daughters had come to see her off. Godwin spoke to her. Yes, she'd be happy to take charge of Mary. "I shall have none of my own daughters with me, and shall therefore have the more leisure to attend to yours."

So Mary was introduced to this motherly woman. The boat prepared to leave. Mary said good-bye to her father and sisters, who scrambled onto the dock. As the *Osnaburgh* slowly pulled away, Mary took a last look at all that was familiar, and with a heart no doubt full of anxiety and anticipation sailed off into the unknown.

The next day, Godwin wrote to William Baxter, anxious about the trouble he was giving him, guilty that he'd foisted his daughter off on him for months "upon so slight an acquaintance." Of course, he knew that the reason Baxter was so willing to accept Mary without having met her was because of her illustrious parents.

Godwin didn't want her "treated with extraordinary attention" on that account or for anyone to go out of their way for her. "I am anxious that she should be brought up (in this respect) like a philosopher," her father wrote. "It will add greatly to the strength and worth of her character."

Except for her arm, he assured Baxter, Mary was strong and healthy with "an excellent appetite." She had "considerable talent," no love of frivolous amusements, "and will be perfectly satisfied with your woods and your mountains."

She was more than satisfied with everything. Mr. Baxter turned out to be a big, friendly, easygoing sort of man. Of his three daughters, the oldest, Margaret, was married. Then came Christy, then Isabel, who was eighteen. Isabel and Mary quickly became best friends, the first real friend Mary had ever had.

The Baxters' large, comfortable house overlooked the water and had a view of the Grampian Mountains. The family took her on sightseeing trips into the Scottish countryside, once to a house that contained a room hung all about with mirrors. Mary stepped in and was immediately surrounded by reflections of heavenly cloud-capped mountains. Enraptured, she fell to her knees in awe.

Along with the beauty of nature, Mary had the privacy and freedom to roam the woods and stride along the shore while her imagination soared. Although her writing was still ordinary and imitative, it didn't matter. "It was beneath the trees of the grounds belonging to our house," she later wrote, "or on the bleak sides of the woodless mountains near, that my true compositions, the airy flights of my imagination, were born and fostered." These daydreams and fictional tales featured impossibly glamorous heroes and heroines, not her ordinary self. Her imagination didn't stretch far enough for her to conceive that "romantic woes or wonderful events would ever be my lot."

Mary stayed in Scotland for five months, then brought Christy, the middle Baxter daughter, home with her to London for a six-month visit. She had a good time showing her guest around and joining in arguments about the role of women with her, Fanny, and Jane. Christy and Fanny thought a woman's place was in the home; Mary and Jane thought not.

On June 3, Mary returned to Scotland for a blissful ten months. During this time, her friend Isabel became engaged to a wealthy older man, her former brother-in-law, David Booth. Mary got permission from her father to prolong her visit to March of 1814. After that, it was time to return to England and her family. In a flurry of last-minute good-byes and promises of eternal friendship, sixteen-year-old Mary Godwin was rowed out to the *Osnaburgh*. Ten days later, she was home.

Mary returned to find that her stepbrother, Charles, now twenty, had moved to Edinburgh, where he was working in a printing house. Twenty-one-year-old Fanny and fifteen-year-old Jane were still at home. William, eleven, was a day pupil at Charterhouse School, several blocks away. Mary's sisters filled her in on some other news: Godwin had a handsome new disciple—Percy Bysshe Shelley. He was twenty-one, a poet, and the son of a wealthy baronet. Mary may have remembered meeting him and his wife on her previous visit home.

Since then, Shelley had become a frequent visitor. He and Godwin sat up for hours discussing radical philosophy. He'd also promised to give Godwin money to pay off his pressing debts, because although the bookstore seemed to be flourishing, the Godwins' finances were their usual mess. Shelley was out of town now but due back in a few months. The news could hardly have been of much interest to Mary. What had she to do with a married man?

Mary had read her mother's last, unfinished novel, *Maria, or The Wrongs of Woman,* written in the form of a mother telling her young daughter her life story. How could she not have seen it but as her own mother's letter to her? The mother in the novel warns her daughter not to let "the spring-tide of existence pass away, unimproved, unenjoyed.—Gain experience—ah! gain it—while experience is worth having, and acquire sufficient fortitude to pursue your own happiness . . . ." It was advice Mary was perfectly willing to follow, but what great experience, what happiness, would she find back in stale old, same old Skinner Street?

What her sisters may not have told Mary was that Percy Bysshe Shelley was beautiful—great staring blue eyes, a tangle of fair curly hair. Or that his emotions darted across his delicate features like quicksilver. Or that he had high ideals, a soaring imagination, and an aching need for a woman who could satisfy his soul.

FIVE

Prince Charming

. . . beautiful and ineffectual angel, beating in the void his luminous wings in vain.

—from *The Study of Poetry* by Matthew Arnold

In 1792, five years before Mary Godwin was born into a London circle of freethinking radicals, Percy Bysshe Shelley had been born into a Jane Austen world of quiet country estates and conservative ideas. He grew up at Field Place, the family estate near Horsham, in Sussex. His forty-year-old father, Sir Timothy, was a Whig squire, a conservative and conformist, who loved and was proud of his oldest son but hadn't a clue to understanding him. Shelley grew up happy at home, surrounded by and dominating his four adoring little sisters. He and Elizabeth, the sister closest to him in age, wrote poetry together. At ten, he wrote his first poem, five stanzas about "A Cat in Distress," the same age Mary had been when she wrote "Mounseer Nongtongpaw."

He was given a conventional gentleman's upbringing: Syon House boarding school at ten; then Eton, a famous

41

public grammar school, where he studied mainly Latin, Greek, a little Hebrew, writing, and arithmetic; then Oxford University.

At Syon House, Shelley developed his lifelong passion for astronomy, magnetism, and electricity—all kinds of science. Dr. Adams Walker, a traveling lecturer and inventor, taught him how to use the telescope and microscope. Shelley peered up at stars and planets (he was sure Saturn was inhabited), down at mites and the wings of flies. He loved the idea of science as power and dreamed of how electricity would change the world. A schoolmate said he "not infrequently" blew up "the boundary palings of the playground with gunpowder, also the lid of his desk in the middle of schooltime, to the great surprise of . . . the whole school."

At home, his sisters trembled before him. Hellen's heart failed her whenever he came toward them with "his piece of folded brown packing-paper under his arm and a bit of wire and a bottle." Before she knew it, "we were placed hand-in-hand round the nursery table to be electrified."

A frail, excitable boy, tall, thin, and awkward, he was a natural target. The other boys at school made his life "a perfect hell," cornering and baiting him like a mad bull until he screamed with rage. They called him "Mad Shelley." "Shelley! Shelley! Shelley!" they'd yell, hundreds of boys' voices echoing through the stone hallways. They'd knock his books from his arms and pull at his hair and clothes as he bent to pick them up. Once he became so angry he plunged a penknife into another boy's hand. For consolation, he read Gothic romances and horror novels, sixpence each in blue paper covers, immersing himself in a world of haunted castles, murderers, and thieves. He read Matthew "Monk" Lewis' *Tales of Terror* till it was battered and worn, and drew pictures of devils, horned monsters, and other grotesque creatures in the margins. Bad dreams haunted him, and he walked in his sleep.

Shelley's love of science mingled with his love of the occult. He read about witchcraft and magic. One night he tried to raise a ghost by following the directions in a book. He chanted the secret words, then sped across the fields clutching a skull in his hands, sure, from the rustling of the grass behind him, that the devil was at his heels. At the church near his father's house was a vault containing the bones of dead bodies. He yearned to spend a night there, fearful but thrilled at the possibility of seeing the dead rise.

When he was eighteen, he wrote and published a Gothic novel called *Zastrozzi: A Romance* and published it along with his first volume of poetry, cowritten with Elizabeth, and a melodrama in verse. The next year, he published another Gothic novel and another volume of poems. None of it was much good.

Even as a little boy, Shelley saw and hated the hypocrisy of adults. At school, he'd learned to detest bullies and tyrants. A teacher at Eton, Dr. James Lind, introduced him to such books as Tom Paine's *The Rights of Man,* Wollstonecraft's *A Vindication of the Rights of Woman,* and Godwin's *Political Justice.* He adopted Godwin's anarchist philosophy—abolish governments and distribute wealth equally to produce a just, crime-free world.

When Shelley traveled to Oxford to begin his first term, his father, Sir Timothy, escorted him. In Sir Timothy's world, young gentlemen sowed their wild oats by seducing servants and shopgirls. He told his son that he expected him to fool around—he'd even provide for any bastards—but he wasn't to end up married to some lower-class girl. To Shelley, who dreamed of an ideal love, his Christian gentleman of a father seemed a disgusting, unfeeling hypocrite.

Sir Timothy, bursting with pride in his only son, so clever and literary, didn't notice Shelley's reaction. As soon as they reached Oxford, he brought him to the city's leading bookseller. (In those days, booksellers were also printers and publishers.) "My son here," he said, "has a literary turn; he is already an author and do pray indulge him in his printing freaks."

In Shelley's time, academic standards at Oxford were a joke. The few men wealthy enough to attend didn't have to work hard. University life was like a pleasant club where young men dabbled at the classics but otherwise enjoyed themselves drinking, entertaining, and taking in the sporting life of the town.

Shelley found Oxford conservative and dull. Stifled by its atmosphere, he went his own way. He wore his hair long when others wore theirs short. He read for sixteen hours a day in a room crammed with books and scientific apparatus, then curled up on the fireside rug for a four-hour nap, woke, talked to friends, and conducted scientific experiments for the rest of the night.

His friend Thomas Jefferson Hogg, whom he met at Oxford, remembered him turning the handle on the electric generator in his room till sparks shot out and his long hair stood on end, talking excitedly on and on of the power of electricity, thunder, and lightning, of the kites he would make to draw electricity down from the sky.

Shelley and Hogg were constantly together, egging each other on, studying in each other's rooms, taking long walks in the countryside, reading their favorite radical writers, discussing ideas, and sailing paper boats. Although Shelley convinced Hogg that he should fall in love with his sister Elizabeth (sight unseen), she had no interest in falling in love with him.

After hours of discussion, Shelley had decided that he hated Christianity and that there was no proof of God's existence. With Hogg's help, he wrote a pamphlet, *The Necessity of Atheism,* which he printed anonymously. Some copies he sent to bishops and the heads of colleges; others he took around to the nearest bookseller and stacked them in his shop window. Twenty minutes later, a teacher at one of the colleges passed the window, saw the pamphlet, read it, and ordered the bookseller to burn every copy in the store except for the one he took to the authorities.

Shelley's pamphlet was almost the first known assertion of atheism printed in England, not a country where freedom of thought in religion had ever been encouraged. (England's insistence on religious conformity was one reason why the recently formed United States, remembering English laws, had made freedom of religion part of the First Amendment to the Constitution it had passed a few years before.) Shelley could have been arrested for criminal behavior. He could have been, and almost was, prosecuted for blasphemy. Despite the pamphlet's anonymous author, Shelley's views were known; it wasn't difficult to figure out who had written it.

Shelley had clearly intended to provoke, so it's difficult to understand his shock when he was called up before the university authorities and expelled. He ran to Hogg's room, sat on the sofa, and burst out over and over, "Expelled! Expelled!" Hogg went to protest his friend's expulsion. For his pains he got himself expelled too. The two young men slunk away to London, where they rented a small dark room. Shelley wrote his father and told him what had happened.

Shelley and Hogg went to see Sir Timothy, who was so upset that he couldn't speak coherently. His only son, his heir, his clever boy of whom he'd been so proud—an atheist! Expelled! He scolded, he cried, he swore, he wept. Shelley, perched on the edge of his chair, suddenly erupted into wild, demonic laughter, slid backward, and lay stretched out full length on the floor. Sir Timothy had no sympathy for hysteria. Shelley must return home and be purged of his "diabolical and wicked" opinions by a tutor of Sir Timothy's choosing. Shelley refused.

Sir Timothy ceased talking to his son except through a lawyer. To retaliate, Shelley said he was renouncing his claim to the estate. He'd take an annuity of 2,000 pounds instead. This was a low blow. To men of Sir Timothy's class, nothing was more important than passing an estate down from father to eldest son. Shelley had his radicalism and his high ideals to sustain him, but his father, who understood neither, felt rejected. He finally agreed to give Shelley an allowance of 200 pounds a year.

While in London, Shelley visited his sisters at boarding school, where he met one of their friends, fifteen-year-old

Harriet Westbrook, pink-cheeked and pretty, with lots of curly hair. Enthralled by Shelley, she adopted his political views, defying her school and family to be with him.

Like his heroes Godwin and Wollstonecraft, Shelley didn't believe in marriage. Love should be free. The present system of marriage, he said, turned married women into high-class prostitutes. Besides, it was impossible to be faithful, "even to an excellent spouse." It would be better to abolish marriage; "inheritance through the female line and children brought up by their mothers, financially supported by the state if necessary, would be a far better system."

But in the present imperfect world, he realized, the burden of free love fell on women, who became scandals and outcasts if they lived with a man without marrying him. And after all, even Godwin and Wollstonecraft had married. So despite his beliefs and his father's disapproval, Shelley and Harriet ran off to Scotland and married. Hogg, who soon moved in with them, tried to seduce Harriet. Because Shelley believed that love shouldn't be exclusive, he was perfectly willing to share. Harriet, however, said no.

Then Shelley got an amazing piece of news: William Godwin was alive. The formerly famous Godwin had been living in such obscurity that Shelley had assumed he was dead. Now he shot off a letter to his idol, expressing his profound admiration and asking to meet him. A meeting was arranged, and they hit it off at once, though Shelley was astonished when the great defender of equality asked him why he'd sent his letter to plain "Mr." Godwin instead of to "William Godwin, Esquire," the proper way a gentleman should be addressed.

Although Godwin was an outcast in respectable society, Shelley was not the first young radical to seek him out. His disciples were attracted to him because, underneath his cold, middle-aged exterior, he was sympathetic and still held fast to the principles of his youth. Other freethinkers' ardor for the ideals of the French Revolution had been quenched after the Reign of Terror, when thousands had died under the guillotine. But Godwin could overlook the acts of murderous terrorists; for him, the crimes of individuals were but "specks on the sun."

Another principle that Godwin still hung on to was that money was meant to be shared. Just because money happened to be in your possession didn't mean that it belonged to you. If others needed it more, you should give it to them. He lived his philosophy. Aaron Burr had noted that the Godwins wouldn't let him repay some money he'd borrowed from them. "Mr. and Mrs. Godwin would not give me their account," Burr wrote, "which must be five or six pounds; a very serious sum to them; they say that, when I succeed in the world, they will call on me for help."

Of course if *you* needed money and other people had it, they were required to give it to you. Godwin didn't go so far as to say that you should *take* what you needed, but you were certainly justified in going after it in any way you could. And because Godwin was more often in need of money than otherwise, his was a convenient philosophy to have.

Shelley accepted it fully. In his eyes, Godwin was a great man and a profound thinker unjustly ignored by society. Shelley felt that it was his duty to help him in any way possible. Godwin agreed. Shelley had little money himself, but he could "borrow on his expectations," as it was called. When his father died and he came into his inheritance, the loan would be repaid. He began negotiations for one of these post-obit (from *post obitum,* "after death") loans at once.

Conversations with Godwin were the one bright spot in Shelley's life. His marriage to Harriet had deteriorated. When their daughter, Ianthe, was born, Harriet refused to nurse her as Shelley wished. Harriet's older sister Eliza had moved in. Shelley thought Harriet was too much under her sister's thumb. The young couple agreed to separate temporarily. In the spring of 1814, Shelley stayed for awhile at the country home of a woman friend, Mrs. Boinville, and her daughter, Cornelia. Although he wasn't in love with Cornelia, seeing and talking to her made him realize what was missing in his relationship with his wife: "the mildness, the intelligence, the delicacy of a cultivated female."

He was sick of Harriet. Being married to her "felt as if a dead and living body had been linked together in loathsome and horrible communion." And he was stuck. Except under the most difficult, expensive, and time-consuming conditions, divorce in early nineteenth-century England was impossible.

One day, Shelley set out on a long walk from Mrs. Boinville's house to his father's, some forty miles away. As he walked, he let his imagination roam. What if he were to meet another woman, the ideal lover about whom he had always fantasized? He imagined their meeting and their declarations of love; he imagined them overcoming the hurdles in their path. He had reached the point of composing a letter to Harriet telling her that he loved someone else, when he came to his senses. His ideal woman was a dream. His "loathsome and horrible communion" with Harriet, unfortunately, was a reality.

In May, he left the Boinvilles and returned to London. On the fifth, he had dinner with the Godwins, whose sixteen-year-old daughter Mary had recently come home.

SIX

Romance

How beautiful and calm and free thou wert
  In thy young wisdom, when the mortal chain
  Of Custom thou didst burst and rend in twain,
And walked as free as light the clouds among. . . .

—from the dedication to *The Revolt of Islam*
by Percy Bysshe Shelley

On May 5, 1814, Mary and Shelley sat down together at her family's dinner table. They had met once before between her two visits to Scotland, but she had been a girl of fifteen then, he a married man in the company of his wife. Now she was a young woman, a few months shy of seventeen. He was twenty-one, unhappily married, and alone.

Shelley looked at Mary and saw the daughter of Mary Wollstonecraft and William Godwin, his two idols. More than that, he saw his dream vision made flesh—a delicate young woman, gentle, pale, and slender with a halo of light reddish-brown hair and a soft, persuasive, almost pathetic smile. Mary looked at Shelley and saw the handsome prince of the fairy-tales she had read as a child.

Both saw each other through the filter of their dreams and desires. Mary gazed at Shelley's fair, angelic face under its mop of unruly curls as he, flushed with joy and exaltation, spoke of a world where liberty ruled and misery and evil were vanquished. These were the same ideas and beliefs her beloved father had taught her all her life, but spoken now through a young man's ardent lips, his voice eloquent, his blue eyes staring and wild. She responded to his words, stunning him with her originality and intelligence. Behind her delicacy he saw a brilliant mind, a streak of wildness, a hatred of injustice that matched his own.

They also saw each other through the romantic atmosphere of their times. Romanticism, which flourished from the late eighteenth century through the early nineteenth, was first of all an artistic, musical, and literary style, and Shelley himself would become one of its greatest poets. But it was also a way of being and feeling. Romantics, spurning what they perceived as the often artificial constraints of eighteenth-century art and life, valued emotion more than reason, the heart above the head. A favorite word was *sensibility*—the ability to respond feelingly to the beauty of nature and the sorrows of other human beings. The character Marianne in Jane Austen's *Sense and Sensibility* is a Romantic. Above all, Romantics valued imagination—the capacity to infuse the world as it actually is with a vision of how it might be, a freeing of the unconscious mind, a belief in dreams.

The books Mary and Shelley both loved to read were Romantic novels—melodramatic Gothic fictions full of plaintive heroines, dashing heroes, promises of eternal fidelity, tears, wild threats, and desperate acts. Inevitably, unknowingly, Mary and Shelley began to fall in love. Without realizing it, they would shape the words, feelings, and actions of their love affair to fit the patterns of the Romantic age.

Shelley was in and out of the house often in the following few weeks, discussing the loan he was trying to negotiate for himself and Godwin. Mary sat upstairs in the schoolroom with her sisters, reading, writing, talking, doing needlework—knowing that Shelley was in her father's study underneath—and waiting until his footsteps sounded on the old wooden steps and he bounded into the schoolroom, ready to talk and talk.

One afternoon when her father was out and she didn't expect to see Shelley, Mary heard his voice from downstairs calling out, "Where is Godwin?" She ran to the door and softly opened it.

"Shelley!" she cried. Another young man stood next to him. Shelley didn't introduce his companion, just answered, "Mary!" and pulled her from the room. They had a few moments' whispered conversation as she told him her father was away.

The young man was Thomas Jefferson Hogg. Shelley had dropped in to give his best friend a chance to see Mary, though he didn't say so. Hogg had been struck by the young woman's piercing look and by her quietness and paleness. "Who was that, pray?" he asked as they continued their walk along Holborn, "A daughter?"

"Yes," Shelley answered.

"A daughter of William Godwin?"

"The daughter of Godwin and Mary."

As May turned to June and the weather grew warmer, Shelley and Mary went for long afternoon walks. They strolled the grounds of nearby Charterhouse School or visited Mary Wollstonecraft's tomb in the old St. Pancras churchyard. Jane accompanied them on their walks, but luckily for Mary and Shelley's desire for privacy, Fanny was away on a visit to Wales. It was easier to get rid of a fifteen-year-old sister than a vigilant older one. "Why don't you walk ahead," Mary suggested to Jane. "We're talking philosophy. You wouldn't be interested." Jane, who cared nothing about philosophy, was happy to leave them to themselves.

No doubt, as younger sisters will, she eavesdropped from time to time. But if she did, she heard nothing more than the philosophical discussions she despised. Although Mary and Shelley had fallen deeply in love, neither acknowledged it.

Shelley tried to pretend that what he felt for Mary was friendship and affection. He was, after all, a married man. Although temporarily separated from Harriet, he planned to rejoin her as soon as his financial problems were settled. She was his wife, despite all his talk of loathsome unions of the living and the dead. They had a child, and she was pregnant with another. Besides, even if he disregarded his duty to his wife, he shrank from declaring himself to Mary. With no chance of divorce, all he could offer her was a life of sin and scandal. A young woman of sixteen, no matter how unconventional her family, could not have a love affair with a married man without ruining her reputation.

Throughout June, Mary and Shelley walked and talked of philosophy and fell more and more in love. On the beautiful Sunday evening of June 26, the elder Godwins went out to visit friends for tea. Mary, Shelley, and Jane decided to walk to St. Pancras. Twilight came as they reached the churchyard. The air was calm, the sky clear. Ten years later, Mary would still recall "the lamplike moon" hanging in the heavens, "the dye of sunset" in "the bright west." While Jane wandered among the gravestones, Shelley and Mary sat beside her mother's tomb and talked.

It was their longest, most personal talk so far. He told her about his childhood. Sitting so close to her in the deepening twilight, talking in hushed tones, Shelley grew agitated. He stumbled for words as he told Mary how he felt about her—half saying it, half denying what he was saying, talking of love, duty, obligations—all a terrible jumble of passion and guilt.

Mary stopped him, sweeping his objections away. She loved him, she said, as much as he loved her. His anxieties, his fears were illusions. Love was supreme and should be free. What was the point of living a lie? *Adultery, infidelity*—they were mere words, "vulgar superstitions" that mustn't be allowed to contaminate their "pure and sacred" love. Shelley quieted. She was right. Mary's spirit had seen "into the truth of things."

Neither ever forgot that moment when each admitted "I love you." The "rapturous moment when she confessed herself mine," Shelley called it, and said it was his true birthday. For Mary, it was the time when "first love shone in your dear eyes"—a vision that remained with her all her life.

Wrapped in love and delusions, they spent the following week secretly discussing plans. They couldn't stay in

England, where Mary would be a social outcast, so they would live in Switzerland instead. All they had to do was get Shelley's wife and Mary's father to agree. Mary suggested that Harriet, who perhaps did have some claim on Shelley, could live with them "as a sister." They'd discuss the idea when she arrived in London. As for Godwin, Mary was sure he'd recognize that she was simply acting on the ideas he'd taught her. As soon as negotiations for the loan were complete, Shelley would inform Godwin of their plans.

On July 6, Shelley finally signed for a post-obit loan of 2,600 pounds, of which 1,100 was for Godwin, the money to be available in two weeks. That afternoon after dinner, Mary waited at home while Shelley took Godwin for a walk to tell him that he and Mary were in love and planned to go to Switzerland to live.

Godwin returned from the walk furious and ordered Mary to her room, refusing to talk to her. He forbade Shelley to come to the house. Mary and Shelley had seriously miscalculated her father's reaction. As the father of a sixteen-year-old girl seduced by a married man who had been a guest in his home, he felt outraged and betrayed. On the other hand, as a great but misunderstood and wrongfully maligned philosopher, he felt he was still entitled to Shelley's money. To Godwin, his money and his daughter were two separate issues. It never occurred to him to refuse his share of Shelley's loan.

Angry, miserable, and confused, Mary was confined to her room for two days until her father summoned her to his study. If she expected that he would simply forbid her to see Shelley, she was wrong. Godwin knew that she could always find some way to run off with her lover if she wanted to. So he had to appeal to her reason, convince her that she must give Shelley up.

He began by pointing out that Shelley had been selfish, thinking only of himself. He'd seduced her with no regard for the fact that now she'd be an outcast in other people's eyes.

But he didn't seduce her, Mary argued. It had been as much her idea as his. Besides, she didn't care what other people thought.

But, her father continued, she was also encouraging him to abandon his wife and child. That's what Gilbert Imlay had done to her mother, and what did she think of him?

Mary's only answer had to be that Shelley loved her.

But he'd forget about her if she discouraged him, Godwin said. Harriet was on her way to London. When she and Shelley met, they might work out their differences and get back together.

Besides, Godwin went on, striking the one note she couldn't resist, she should think of what she was doing to her family. Causing a scandal would only tarnish her mother's memory further. And she was torturing him, emotionally and financially. He was headed for ruin if the deal with Shelley didn't go through. He still hadn't received that 1,100 pounds—and Shelley had promised more in the future. She had to give up Shelley and let things go back to the way they were.

Worn down, in awe of her father, and guilt-ridden over her family obligations, Mary gave in and agreed not to see Shelley anymore. She would sacrifice her own happiness to do what was right and brave. She would never love another, she knew, but she would give up Shelley. Godwin had her write a letter telling Shelley her decision. She promised not to leave the house.

A few days later, as Mary sat in the schoolroom, expecting never again to hear Shelley's feet bounding up the stairs, the porter who worked in the bookshop handed her a small package that Shelley had bribed him to deliver. With trembling hands, she opened it. Beneath the wrappings was a copy of *Queen Mab,* a book of poetry Shelley had published several years before, containing the most radical statements of his ideas.

Mary opened the book and read her name—*Mary Wollstonecraft Godwin*—inscribed in Shelley's handwriting. (The original dedication, printed in the book, was to Harriet.) A note from Shelley fell out. True to her promise to her father, she didn't reply to the note. But no promise kept her from writing her feelings into the book itself where no one would ever see. This was as close to her beloved as she might ever be again. She took out her pen and on the book's endpapers wrote:

> This book is sacred to me and as no other creature shall ever look into it, I may write in it what I please—yet what shall I write, that I love the author beyond all power of expression and that I am parted from him. Dearest and only love by that love we have promised to each other although I may not be yours I can never be another's.
>
> But I am thine exclusively thine—by the kiss of love by

(And here she quoted a few lines from Byron's poem "To Thyrza.")

I have pledged myself to thee and sacred is the gift—

I remember your words, *you are now Mary going to mix with many and for a moment I shall depart but in the solitude of your chamber I shall be with you*—yes you are ever with me, sacred vision.

Meanwhile, Shelley, desperate, ranted and raved to his friends about how cruel it was to keep him tied to the woman he despised and separated from the one he loved. "Every one who knows me must know that the partner of my life should be one who can feel poetry and understand philosophy." He waved a bottle of laudanum, a powerful, potentially lethal drug. "Harriet is a noble animal, but she can do neither."

Less than a week after Mary's renunciation, Harriet arrived in London. She was nineteen and pregnant with her second child. Shelley browbeat her into agreeing to a separation. Now, he thought, all would be well. He took Harriet with him to Skinner Street so she could see the Godwins and tell them her decision in person. He even suggested that she call on Mary to comfort her during this difficult time. This Harriet refused to do. She also turned down the idea of living with Shelley and Mary "as a sister."

In fact, Harriet had no intention of giving Shelley up. She went to the Godwins alone, upset and crying, and begged Godwin to keep the lovers apart. She begged Mary to write to Shelley words that would calm him and subdue his love for her. Mary assured her that she'd keep her promise and not give in to Shelley's pleas.

On July 19, Godwin finally received his 1,100 pounds from Shelley's loan. He could rest easy now. He had his money and his daughter. Jane and Mary were still confined to the house. He planned to send Mary abroad to live with friends for a while and be out of Shelley's reach.

But Shelley refused to give up. One afternoon, Mary and Jane were in the schoolroom when they heard shouting from downstairs and hurried footsteps, then Shelley burst in, Mrs. Godwin on his heels, both shouting. Shelley dashed up to Mary, his great blue eyes wild and staring. He held a bottle of laudanum in his hand.

"They wish to separate us, my beloved; but Death shall unite us." He offered her the bottle. "By this you can escape from tyranny." He pulled a small pistol from his pocket and pointed it at himself. "And this shall reunite me to you."

Jane screamed and shrieked. Mary turned pale. Tears streaming down her cheeks, she begged Shelley to calm himself, to go home. "I won't take this laudanum," she told him, "but if you will only be reasonable and calm, I will promise to be ever faithful to you." Mary's words and manner cooled him down. Once the melodramatic scene had run its course, Shelley left the house.

Despite Mary's good intentions to keep her promise to her father and Harriet, she continued to read the letters Shelley bribed the shop porter to smuggle in to her. In them, he did everything he could to change her mind. Unless she joined him as the partner of his life, he wrote, he'd destroy himself.

She believed him. There had already been rumors from the hotel where he was staying of his swallowing some laudanum and of his friends having to walk him around the streets until it wore off. She didn't know what to do. Writing to her kept his hopes alive and prevented him from accepting his loss. But the only way to stop him from sending her letters was to tell her father, and she feared that if Godwin stopped the correspondence, Shelley would surely kill himself.

Besides, his passion and persistence were wearing her down. And she did love him. Yes, she finally wrote to him, she would do as he asked. She would come to him and they would run away.

SEVEN

Adventure

When peace came, after many long years of war,
when our island prison was opened to us, and our
watery exit from it was declared practicable, it was
the paramount wish of every English heart, ever
addicted to vagabondizing, to hasten to the continent. . . ; a new generation had sprung up, and the
whole of this, who had money and time at com-
mand, poured, in one vast stream, across the Pas
de Calais into France.

> —from an article in *Westminster Review* (1826)
> by Mary Shelley

Once Mary had made up her mind to run away, planning the elopement became an adventure. They decided that Shelley would hire a carriage and meet her at 4
A.M. at the corner of Holborn and Hatton Garden on July
28. From there, they would flee to France and then to
Switzerland.

When Jane got wind of their plans, she begged to go along. She'd be a help, she said, because she could speak French better than they could. No doubt she realized that once Mary left, all excitement and drama would drain away from Skinner Street, leaving only rules and restrictions in their wake. Besides—to see France! Mary found it hard to refuse her. Hadn't Jane stood by her throughout her ordeal? If it was all right with Shelley, Jane could come too.

Mary packed with the idea that, so far as she knew, she was never coming home again. All her most precious papers went into her trunk—letters from Shelley, her father, her friends, all her writings. She penned a quick note to her father and left it on his dressing table. Then the two girls put on their black silk traveling dresses and bonnets and crept out the shop door onto Skinner Street in the hour just before dawn.

Mary ran down the block to where Shelley waited with the carriage. Was it all right with him if Jane came too? Yes, that was fine. They went back to get Jane and the luggage and they were off, speeding toward Dover on the English coast.

At Dartford, they took on four fresh horses to "outstrip pursuit," as Shelley said, as though he imagined Godwin, booted and spurred, galloping hot on their heels. They gripped the sides of the coach as it rattled onward, flinging them against its sides, the dust of the road spurting out behind. It was wild and exciting, a tremendous lark, for two teenage girls of fifteen and sixteen and an impassioned young poet of twenty-one, running away from the dreariness and respectability of conventional adult society toward a new world of freedom and love.

Back in London, a few hours after dawn, Godwin woke and read the note on his dressing table. He had no intention of pursuing his runaway daughter. He had brought her up to be honest and truthful and to keep her promises. She had broken her word. She had betrayed him. His heart hardened against her. He intended never to speak to her again.

As the sunny July day wore on, heat built up inside the small coach. Mary felt ill and they had to keep stopping to let her rest. In the afternoon, some twelve hours after they started out, they reached Dover. Here they had to deal with the customs house, arrange for transportation, and get something to eat. It was 6 P.M. when they stepped into a small boat for what should have been a two-hour sail across the English Channel.

For the first time that day, they could relax. It was a beautiful evening. The boat pushed off, and the sails flapped in the slight breeze. But as the moon rose and darkness fell, a wind sprang up. The waves mounted higher, tossing the boat. Shelley, who loved boats and sailing, was in his element, but Mary was so seasick she huddled between Shelley's knees, her head close against his chest.

The wind grew stronger. Hour after hour throughout the night, the boat jounced about on the rough seas. A storm blew up. Lightning flashed. A thunder squall struck the boat, and waves poured in over the sides. Mary was too sick to realize the danger they were in. At last the wind shifted and drove them forward to the port at Calais. By the time the boat drove onto the sand, Mary had fallen asleep. The wind calmed as the sky grew light. Shelley bent over her sleeping form. "Mary look," he whispered, "the sun rises over France."

The three travelers scrambled from the boat and walked together across the sand to an inn. Shelley and Mary had decided to keep a journal, a joint record of their new life together, in which they would take turns writing what they saw, felt, did, read, and thought. Once safely inside their rented rooms, Shelley picked up the green notebook they were using and wrote, "Mary was there." Mary took the pen from his hand and added, "Shelley was also with me." What more did they need?

They stayed at the inn all that day, recovering from their voyage and awaiting their luggage, which had crossed on a separate boat. That evening, the captain of their boat told them they had a visitor—a fat lady who claimed that Shelley had run off with her daughter. It was Mrs. Godwin in pursuit of her darling Jane.

Mrs. G. hustled her daughter into her room. All night she sat up with her, begging her to come home. In the morning, Jane came into Mary and Shelley's room and announced that she was returning. Her mother's pleas and tears had worn her down.

That was a big decision, Shelley said. Maybe she should take half an hour to think it over.

Jane didn't need half an hour. Shelley's suggestion was enough. She hurried back to her mother to say she was staying after all. Mrs. Godwin, with no more to say, returned to England in defeat.

The boat with the luggage arrived, and the three adventurers set off on their journey through France, a country they'd only read about in books. To young English people of Mary and Jane's generation, shut up on their own little island throughout the long years of the

Napoleonic Wars, the world across the English Channel seemed exotic and far away. Now peace was at hand. What could be more fun than to traipse across foreign lands?

Nothing was inconvenient or annoying, only amusing—even the ordeal of passing through the customs house—because it was a new experience. The descriptions of themselves written in their passports delighted them. They were ecstatic over the strange, foreign clothes Frenchwomen wore. They eagerly examined every new meal placed in front of them, convinced "that the fried-leaves of artichokes were frogs." And miracle of miracles, they heard little boys and girls actually speaking French. It was all "acting a novel, being an incarnate romance."

The practicalities of their journey didn't concern them. Like travelers in old tales, as Mary's biographer Muriel Spark says, or like footloose young people of the 1960s and '70s, they assumed that a place to sleep, food and drink, and the means of getting around would turn up as needed.

Mary had inherited her love for travel from her mother. Mary Wollstonecraft had helped set the style for romantic journeys in *Letters Written During a Short Residence in Sweden, Norway and Denmark,* containing letters she'd sent to her lover Imlay during a trip to Scandinavia. She had traveled to France in the heady days of the French Revolution. Switzerland may have been Mary and Shelley's destination because it was the place her mother had always wanted to see. (Also, as radicals, they would rather live in a republic like Switzerland than under the reactionary monarchy that had been reinstated in France.)

Now Mary Wollstonecraft's daughter was trying to re-trace her footsteps—and her life. Mary had brought her mother's books with her, and she and Shelley read them aloud to each other along the way, starting with *Mary: A Fiction,* a semi-autobiographical novel written when Wollstonecraft was in her late twenties. In it she implies that acting as one feels is better than blindly obeying the rules. It may have cheered Mary to think that her mother wouldn't have blamed her for following her heart and eloping with a married man.

Shelley, as fascinated by Mary's mother as she was, and drawn to Mary partly because she was her mother's daughter, was eager to know whether she shared her mother's genius. He asked to see what Mary had written before they met. She showed him the writings she'd brought with her. He glanced through them, and Mary promised to let him read these "productions of her mind" thoroughly once they were settled in Switzerland.

He had no time to read them now. They had reached Paris, but their money was running low. He would have to try to borrow some from a moneylender. In the mean-time, they were prisoners in the city without the cash to move on. To cheer Shelley up, Mary read him some passages from the poems of Lord Byron, then England's most famous poet.

Shelley was finally able to obtain the funds they needed and, almost a week after their arrival, they set off through the countryside. In the excitement and confusion of leaving Paris, Mary's trunk with her letters and writings was accidentally left behind. It was never recovered.

To make their money last, they decided to walk from

Paris to Switzerland, some 250 miles—a wild scheme that only very young people would have dared to undertake. They bought a mule to carry their luggage—or Mary or Jane when they grew tired. Less than a hundred miles into their journey, Shelley sprained his ankle, and they rode the rest of the way in a cart.

During their journey, Mary got a close look at the devastation of war, including entire villages that had been completely destroyed. She later wrote:

> The distress of the inhabitants whose houses had been burnt; their cattle killed, and all their wealth destroyed, has given a sting to my detestation of war, which none can feel who have not travelled through a country pillaged and wasted by this plague, which, in his pride, man inflicts upon his fellow.

Growing up in London, she'd been little touched by the war. At first it had been fought only at sea. As it came closer to home, it was felt mainly outside of London and by the poor, as men were drafted, prices rose, food grew scarce, and soldiers were everywhere underfoot.

Her Grandmother Godwin, living in the country, had felt the war's impact more than city people did. "What do you think of the war?" she had written to her son in 1801. "O what scarcity of bread and all kinds of provision. Malt 44 shillings per comb; and the poor, some starving, some stealing, though wages increased, and parish allowance. Sin is certainly the cause of calamity."

Hard times continued even as the war came to an end. In France, poverty was everywhere. Farm workers didn't earn enough to feed themselves and their families. Town workers, at home and in factories, worked terribly long hours for low wages. In Paris, housing was scarce and conditions decidedly unsanitary. Mary complained that people were often rude to them, perhaps forgetting that to the French they represented the enemy who had defeated them.

The inns where they stayed were often filthy. Rats kept Jane awake one entire night. She said she could feel their cold paws on her face. But she rested on the bed with Mary and Shelley, feeling safe there. Shelley was her protector—when men made indecent proposals to her, Shelley drove them off. But she must have felt very much the outsider, the fifth wheel rumbling along in the company of two people so very much in love.

For Mary, rats in the bed, poor food, dirty rooms, rude people, lack of money, the intrusions of Jane, even the loss of her writings, were only minor annoyances. She was in love and adventuring and having a wonderful time.

They weren't often serious. Shelley liked to tease. Once on the road, Shelley wanted to stop to bathe in a mountain stream. He asked Mary to join him. The bank would shelter her from sight. No, it was indecent, she said, and besides, she had no towel. He said he'd gather leaves and she could dry herself with those. No, she said, mock indignant. How could he think of such a thing?

At the town of Champlitte-et-le-Prélot they made friends with a little girl named Marguerite Pascal. "I never beheld so lovely a child," Mary wrote, and said they would have taken her with them if her father would have allowed it.

Only the thought of her own father spoiled Mary's bliss. Whenever she thought of his rejection, her mood would darken. One evening as she and Jane were laughing over some story, Mary heard herself say something like, "Men were always the sources of a thousand difficulties." Suddenly, she stopped laughing.

"Why do you look so sad?" Shelley asked.

"I was thinking of my father," she said, "and wondering what he was now feeling."

"Do you mean that as a reproach to me?" Shelley asked.

"Oh! No! Don't let us think more about it." But she couldn't help thinking about the rift between herself and the father whom she loved so much, a rift that might never mend. Mrs. Godwin had run after *her* daughter. Godwin hadn't even sent a message asking his daughter to come home.

On August 19 they arrived in Neuchâtel, Switzerland. Mary, who loved mountains so much, got her first view of the Alps—peak after craggy peak of dazzling white extending as far as she could see. The next day, they went to the post office, looking for letters—and money—from friends at home, but found none. Shelley managed to get some money from the bank, but not nearly as much as they would eventually need. They tried unsuccessfully to find transportation to carry them across Switzerland's mountainous terrain.

A friendly Swiss who saw them wandering around town, looking young, helpless, out of place, and speaking French so badly they could hardly make themselves understood, helped them get seats in the coach to Lucerne. He assumed they were runaway lovers. Was he right, he asked—had they escaped from England on account of love? Mary and Shelley said yes. He tried to talk them into returning, but they refused. Then he turned to Jane. Had she run away for the sake of love too?

"Oh! dear no," Jane said. "I came to speak French."

The next day they traveled for more than twelve hours before stopping to spend the night. They'd grown crabby after three weeks on the road. According to Mary, they were "tired of wheeling machines," a much praised cathedral was "very modern and stupid," their room at the inn contained "a horrid spinet and a case of stuffed birds," and Shelley was "in a jocosely, horrible mood." She often felt unwell, probably because she was now pregnant and experiencing morning sickness. Time alone for Shelley and Mary became more precious. The constant companionship of Jane was getting on their nerves.

On August 23, they sailed across Lake Lucerne to Brunnen, where they rented two rooms for six months. The next day they moved in. The reality of their situation hit them. Did they really want to live in this ugly, ill-equipped house, grubbing along on not enough money? There was no point in staying. Their funds had shrunk too low to last for six months. Although Jane pouted, the next day they packed up and traveled back to England by boat along the Rhine River—cheaper than going by land.

On the way home, Shelley finished reading Wollstonecraft's *Mary* aloud and started her *Letters Written During a Short Residence in Sweden, Norway and Denmark.* Mary began to write a novel she called *Hate.* Shelley, who was working on a romance of his own, was pleased that she was writing too. (Unfortunately, this manuscript of Mary's has also been lost.) Not to be left out, Jane was writing a novel called *The Idiot* (*Ideot,* in her spelling). It featured a person whom common people thought an idiot for not conforming "to their vulgar and prejudiced views." It's not difficult to guess on whom her character was based.

Again, sailing back to England, this time across the North Sea from Holland to Gravesend, they were buffeted by a storm. Everyone was seasick except Jane. Finally, on Tuesday, September 13, tired, sick, and bedraggled, they arrived in England with no money to pay the captain. A boat took them up the Thames River to London. Here they hired a coach and then dashed around the city trying to raise money. They tried Shelley's banker, his publisher, and his friends—all without success. At last they went to Harriet. For two hours Mary and Jane huddled together in the coach outside Harriet's house while Shelley haggled with his wife. With the money he finally received, they paid their immediate debts and were able to go to a hotel to rest.

EIGHT

Scandal

I never was attached to that great sect
Whose doctrine is that each one should select
Out of the world a mistress or a friend,
And all the rest, though fair and wise, commend
To cold oblivion. . . .

—from *Epipsychidion* by Percy Bysshe Shelley

M ary and Shelley had come down from their airy balloon ride with a bump. After the fun and adventure of their European jaunt, London offered nothing but pain and anxiety. They were short of money, and Mary was pregnant, an outcast from respectable society. Because she had her own small circle of friends, she didn't much care that other people thought her behavior scandalous. She'd been raised to think for herself, to do what she believed was right despite what society thought. But when David Booth, the husband of her Scottish friend Isabel, sent her a letter saying that he forbade Isabel to write to her, she was badly hurt.

Of her own family, only her stepbrother, Charles Clairmont, was a regular visitor. Her father would have nothing to do with her. One day while out walking with Shelley, Mary saw Charles and her father in the street. She wasn't sure whether he had seen her. When Charles came to visit that evening, she asked if Godwin had seen them. Yes, he said, but had only remarked that it was a shame someone as beautiful as Shelley was so wicked.

Mary's half-sister Fanny visited occasionally, but talked only to Jane. Godwin had threatened never to speak to Fanny again if she talked to Mary. Poor Fanny, torn between her family's warring factions, got little sympathy from anyone. When Mary sent her a lock of her hair, a common memento in those days, Mrs. Godwin punished Fanny by not allowing her to come down to dinner. Mary heard the story from Charles, who kept her posted on Godwin news, noting that "Fanny of course" had behaved "slavishly."

Trying to make sense of her father's attitude, Mary reread *Political Justice*. Hadn't he denounced matrimony? Hadn't he and her mother lived together, unmarried on principle? But Godwin saw nothing in common between his daughter eloping with a married man and his own teachings or actions. Neither he nor Wollstonecraft had been married to anyone else. Besides, his ideas were mere theory. He'd never expected anyone to act on them.

Only his ideas on sharing money were to be taken seriously. Financially, Godwin was in desperate straits. His business was losing money. Creditors were after him. Although he wouldn't meet, speak, or write to the man who'd stolen his daughter, he insisted that Shelley keep his promise to help and continued to pester him for money, using friends as go-betweens.

Godwin's sensitivities can be difficult for anyone but himself to understand. He returned a check to Shelley because Shelley had made it out to *William Godwin* and signed his own name. This "no consideration could induce him to accept." Shelley was to send a duplicate right away made out "to Joseph Hume or James Martin, or any other name in the whole directory," someone who would then cash the check and hand the money over to Godwin.

Shelley had money troubles of his own. Besides himself, Mary and the coming baby, and Jane, he had Harriet, also pregnant, and his daughter Ianthe to provide for. He was badly in debt. Creditors were after him too. In those days, not paying your debts was like fraud or stealing today—you'd cheated your creditors out of their money. If you didn't pay, you went to jail.

Because Shelley was heir to a fortune, he tried to raise money through post-obit loans that would come due when he inherited. While negotiating, he had to keep one jump ahead of his creditors, who were out to arrest him. For more than a month, Mary, Shelley, and Jane moved from place to place as each new address became known. Sometimes they went hungry. Once when they were so strapped that they couldn't pay their landlord, he refused to send up food. They spent hours calling on friends and relations before they finally got something to eat and enough money to pay their bill.

Mary and Shelley dreamed up various ways to get out of their difficulties. Perhaps they could assemble a small group of people and live together in the west of Ireland. Shelley talked of "converting and liberating" two of his sisters from school so they could join too. His friends Thomas Love Peacock, whom he'd met through his publisher two years previously, and Tom Hogg would come, of course, and perhaps Harriet; although for some reason still unclear to him, Harriet had so far declined offers to live with him and Mary. They spent days discussing this impractical plan on their walks—"their running-away scheme," Mary called it.

The dreaded knock on the door came on October 22. Someone had leaked their address, and a creditor was on their doorstep. Shelley was able to give him a little money, enough to satisfy him for the time being. Because it was Sunday, bailiffs, or court officers, weren't allowed to arrest people, so he had a few hours to spend in a frantic, futile scramble to raise more cash.

On Monday Shelley went into hiding; Mary was left alone with Jane to cope. Bailiffs pestered her. She called on friends for help, sold Shelley's microscope for five pounds, and sent him messages at his secret address. When she could, she scuttled off to meet him in coffeehouses and on the street.

At night, she huddled in her room—cold, lonely, and heartsick—writing to Shelley, the one person in the world whose love she could depend on. Her father still refused to see her. Mary blamed his hardness of heart on her stepmother. "I detest Mrs. G. She plagues my father out of his life," she wrote. "Why will not Godwin follow the obvious bent of his affections and be reconciled to us?"

As she formed the words on the page, the bleakness of her life seemed to press down on her. She was only seventeen, with no family to turn to, and worn out from pregnancy and the stress of separation. Once she had been the apple of her father's eye, the delight of friends, the inheritor of her mother's talent and daring. She'd opened up to life, taken risks, and given all to love—as romantically as any heroine in her books or in her dreams.

And now? Her courage slipped. "Goodnight my love," she ended her letter. "Dear good creature, press me to you and hug your own Mary to your heart. Perhaps she will one day have a father. Till then be everything to me, love, and indeed I will be a good girl and never vex you anymore." For a moment, she was a child again, the child whose adored father had gone away. Shelley had become not only her lover but her guide and protector as well.

Their hole-and-corner existence continued for two weeks until Shelley was able to get a loan and they could live together again. A few months later, on January 5, 1815, Shelley's grandfather died and his father inherited. Shelley again offered to give up a portion of the estate he'd receive when his father died in exchange for money now. Negotiations began.

During all this time, Jane had remained with Mary and Shelley despite the hopes of her mother and stepfather that she'd return home. Although she was a runaway, Jane, unlike Mary, was not yet "ruined," that is, she was still a virgin. After a while, the Godwins seemed less eager to take her back, but still anxious to get her out of the clutches of the evil Shelley. Perhaps she could stay in a convent, they thought, or board as a guest in some suitable family, or become a governess.

Jane, who had adopted Shelley's radical theories whole hog, was open to these suggestions with one stipulation:

"that she should in all situations openly proclaim and earnestly support a total contempt for the laws and institutions of society," an attitude unlikely to make her welcome in many convents or homes.

Jane, of course, had no intention of going anywhere. She'd had a taste of freedom and excitement and wasn't about to give them up. In fact, aside from the thrill of outfoxing bailiffs and creditors, life must have seemed drab after her six-week adventure in Europe. To brighten it up, she changed her name. Plain Jane hardly suited her own conception of herself. She changed it to Claire (which she spelled Clare for a while). *Claire Clairmont.* It had a ring to it.

Sixteen-year-old Claire had a great deal of energy and nowhere to channel it. With the household focused on Shelley's debts and Mary's difficult pregnancy, she may have felt neglected and, consciously or not, tried to draw attention, especially Shelley's attention, to herself. Most nights, Mary, easily tired, went to bed early, and Shelley and Claire sat up late, talking of ghosts and other horrors. After one of these talks, Shelley awoke during the night to find Claire in his room, almost hysterical with fright. She asked if he'd touched the pillow near her bed. Of course not, he said. Then the pillow must have moved from a chair to her bed on its own.

Shelley took the shivering, frightened girl back to the sitting room so Mary could sleep. But instead of changing the subject, they continued their spooky conversation till dawn. Claire said that Shelley's face had an expression of "deep sadness and conscious power over her" which terrified her. Soon she was shrieking and writhing on the floor. Shelley had to bring her in to Mary to be calmed down.

Claire had a similar outburst a week later. Shelley began to suspect that these marvelous occurrences had more to do with Claire than with a ghost. The chimney board, he wrote, "is found to have walked leisurely into the middle of the room, accompanied by the pillow; who being very sleepy tried to get into bed again but fell down on his back."

Some people have thought that Claire had a sexual relationship with Shelley, even though he seems to have regarded her less like a lover than like a loved, promising, albeit rather irritating, kid sister. She was a playfellow, an amusing companion, an audience willing to share his love of horrors—someone he could draw into acting out and complementing his own excitable nature. On the other hand, it wouldn't be surprising if two young people living close together felt sexually attracted. Perched on the edge of Mary and Shelley's love affair, living for months within the heated atmosphere of their passion, Claire had undoubtedly developed a crush on the handsome poet whose ideas she idolized but who belonged to the stepsister she had always envied and imitated.

At times Claire and Shelley squabbled. She grew sullen and discontented. He declared her insensitive and incapable of "the slightest degree of friendship." She wrote in her diary, "how hateful it is to quarrel—to say a thousand unkind things—meaning none—things produced by the bitterness of disappointment." Had one or the other of them made a sexual advance and been rejected? "Content yourself with one great affection," Shelley reminded himself.

Mary was tolerant of their relationship, writing one night in her diary, "I go to bed soon—but Shelley and

Jane sit up and for a wonder do not frighten themselves." She knew she didn't have to worry about Shelley's loyalty, for she knew it was herself, deeply passionate but outwardly calm and cool, whom he truly loved. If any three-way love affair were going to develop in their household, it would not be Shelley, Mary, and Claire, but Shelley, Mary, and Hogg.

Thomas Jefferson Hogg had made a habit of falling for Shelley's nearest and dearest female relations, and something in Shelley's nature welcomed the idea of sharing women he loved with his friend. In college they had schemed for Hogg to fall in love with Shelley's sister Elizabeth, whom he hadn't even met. When Shelley was first married, Hogg had made a pass at Harriet. Shelley had grown angry only because Hogg persisted after Harriet refused. Now Shelley was eager for Hogg to know Mary. He'd decided that if Hogg didn't like her, they could no longer be friends. He needn't have worried. On November 14, 1814, Hogg met Mary and promptly fell in love with her. Shelley was thrilled.

Shelley wrapped his feelings in theories. "How you reason and philosophize about love," Mary wrote to him. "Do you know if I had been asked I could not have given one reason in its favor. Yet I have as great an opinion as you concerning its exaltedness and love very tenderly to prove my theory." Mary's theory was simply to express the love she felt for Shelley. His was more complicated. Although he was against promiscuity, sex for sex's sake, he proclaimed that people who loved each other should become intimate whether they were married to other people or not. Love, he declared, should be free, open, and shared.

It was Mary's fate to live with principled men. Like her father, Shelley was forever trying to square his theories with the facts and desires of daily life. Mary was becoming aware of the strange shapes this squaring produced in her father's life. Thomas Love Peacock, she wrote, "has called on my father who will not speak about Shelley to any but an attorney—oh! Philosophy."

Now Mary found herself in a delicate situation. Should she encourage Hogg? She believed that she agreed with Shelley's theories of shared love. Also, as her pregnancy advanced, she often felt left behind. In her journal, she complained, "Very unwell. Shelley and Clary walk out as usual to heaps of places." She also resented Shelley's excitement when, on December 6, Harriet gave birth to a boy, Shelley's "son and heir," as Mary said. Shelley proudly sent off letters announcing the event, which "ought to be ushered in with ringing of bells, etc.," Mary noted bitterly, "for it is the son of his *wife*." So it was pleasant to have Hogg come to talk to her, to keep her company while Claire and Shelley went "hopping about the town," to soothe and flatter her while she was feeling awkward, ill, and out of sorts.

Was there more than that? Years later, when she was an old woman, Claire said she remembered Mary coming to her room, putting her head on her pillow, and crying bitterly, "saying that Shelley wanted her to sleep with Hogg."

Soon Hogg was visiting every evening, staying until 11:30, sometimes all night. During his vacation (he was a lawyer), he stayed the whole time. They became a cozy foursome—Shelley and Claire going on errands and paying visits together, Mary and Hogg together in the evenings, reading, laughing, and talking.

Hogg waited until the first day of 1815 to formally declare his love. Mary replied with delicacy and tact. "You love me you say. I wish I could return it with the passion you deserve. But you are very good to me and tell me you are quite happy with the affection which from the bottom of my heart I feel for you." She pointed out that they'd known each other only a short time and indirectly reminded him she was pregnant. "I was in great pain all night and this morning and am but just getting better." Love would come in time, she promised, "and then"—her insincerity revealed by her sentimental choice of words—"we shall be happier I do think than the angels who sing forever."

Later, she predicted the good times they'd have come summer when the trees turned green and she'd have her little baby. Hogg would teach her Italian and they'd read together, but, she added, and it sounded like a warning, "our still greater happiness will be in Shelley—I who love him so tenderly and entirely, whose life hangs on the beam of his eye and whose whole soul is entirely wrapped up in him, you who have so sincere a friendship for him. . . ." She was letting Hogg know that though she was fond of him and flattered by his passion, Shelley was the emotional center of her life.

The baby Mary carried wasn't due until the end of April. But on February 22, two months too soon, she suddenly felt the sharp cramps that meant labor had begun. The doctor was summoned, but the birth was so quick that the tiny creature, a little girl they named Clara, arrived five minutes before him. Mary was physically in good shape, but exhausted and distressed. The baby wasn't expected to live. Today, a two-months-premature infant would be whisked into an incubator and carefully monitored, but no such resources were available in 1815. Shelley and Mary sat up all night, comforting each other as they waited for the inevitable end. But when dawn broke, little Clara was still alive.

With Godwin out of town, the rest of Mary's family rallied round. Fanny came to be with her sister and stayed all the next night. Even Mrs. Godwin relented far enough to send fresh sheets and other linen with Charles.

On Friday, two-day-old little Clara still lived; she even looked healthier. Mary began to hope. Even the doctor was optimistic. Saturday came. The baby had taken no nourishment since her birth. Was she strong enough to nurse? Mary put her to her breast and Clara began to suck. It looked like she was going to live after all. Shelley and Claire hurried out to get a cradle for this new member of the family and to find a bigger place to live. By Thursday, little Clara was strong enough for them to move to new lodgings, where Mary spent the next few days contentedly reading, talking, and nursing her child.

That Sunday night, after feeding and caring for Clara, Mary went to bed. She awoke during the night to nurse her, but the baby seemed so fast asleep Mary decided not to disturb her. But Clara was not sleeping. Sometime earlier that night she had died, probably from convulsions. In the morning Mary woke up and found her child dead.

Grief overwhelmed her. Shelley feared that she would fall ill. Later that day, reaching out for comfort wherever she could, Mary wrote to Hogg: "My dearest Hogg my baby is dead. Will you come to me as soon as you can."

She explained what had happened. "You are so calm a creature and Shelley is afraid of a fever from the milk—for I am no longer a mother now."

For days Mary continued restless, unhappy, unable to sleep. She struggled against her emotions, for she'd been brought up to be stoic and not dwell on feelings of grief. But her journal entries for the rest of March reveal her misery:

Th. 9. Still think about my little baby. Tis hard indeed for a mother to lose a child.

Mon. 13. Shelley, Hogg, and Clary go to town. Stay at home, net, and think of my little dead baby. This is foolish I suppose, yet whenever I am left alone to my own thoughts and do not read to divert them they always come back to the same point—that I was a mother and am so no longer.

Sun. 19. Dream that my little baby came to life again, that it had only been cold and that we rubbed it by the fire and it lived. I awake and find no baby. I think about the little thing all day.

Mon. 20. Dream again about my baby.

Adding to Mary's misery that spring was her growing irritation at Claire's constant presence. "Very quiet all the morning," she wrote in March, "and happy for Clary does not get up till 4." Although Shelley, disenchanted himself or eager to make Mary happy, was willing for Claire to leave, getting her out was proving impossible. She refused to return to the Godwins, and there seemed no place else. "This is indeed hard to bear," Mary wrote.

Where Claire irritated, Hogg consoled. In March and

April, he spent his six-week holiday with Mary and Shelley. Evidence exists that at this time the two men's wish for a three-way relationship bore fruit. A message from Shelley to Hogg about Mary has survived. In it Shelley speaks of "your share of our common treasure" and of this "exquisite possession," and reassures Hogg that he will not "be deprived of this participated pleasure." Had Mary, in her grief and misery, finally succumbed to Hogg's kindliness and Shelley's plans? No one really knows.

By May, at any rate, Mary was over the worst of her grief. Money matters were settled. After months of negotiating, Shelley and his father signed an agreement. Shelley received several thousand pounds in cash, his debts paid, and an income of 1,000 pounds a year, out of which Harriet got 200 pounds annually and Godwin got 1,000 pounds outright. And Claire, at last, was leaving, moving to the small town of Lynmouth on the coast.

"I begin a new journal with our regeneration," Mary wrote. That new journal, which would relate the events of the year in which she wrote *Frankenstein,* has been lost. The old journal ends with a recipe that Mary jotted down on its inside back cover. Shelley's mind, which always ran to the ghostly and ghoulish, added a recipe of his own: "9 drops of human blood, 7 grains of gunpowder, ½ an oz. of putrified brain, 13 mashed graveworms—the Pecksie's doom salve. The Maie and her Elfin Knight." (Pecksie, the Dormouse, and the Maie were pet names for Mary. She called him the Elfin Knight.) Claire's journal for the next year—the most fateful year of *her* life—has been lost as well.

NINE

Byron and Claire

There be none of Beauty's daughters
With a magic like thee;
And like music on the waters
Is thy sweet voice to me.

—from "There Be None of Beauty's Daughters"
by George Gordon, Lord Byron

With Claire gone, Shelley and Mary decided to rent a house in the country. While Shelley was off house-hunting and taking a dreadfully long time about it, Mary grew more and more lonely and full of unspoken fears. She had gotten rid of Claire all right, but now Shelley was gone, too. She was alone in the house for the first time, perhaps unable to sleep, still mourning the death of her baby. She was also three months pregnant, cause for both joy and fear. She had fits of low spirits as well as a nameless dread—jealousy and suspicion of Claire that she didn't want to admit to, anxiety that Shelley might never return.

She wrote him a long, begging letter. She missed him so *much;* it wasn't right for him to be away so long! She threatened to come after him. "Indeed, my love, I cannot bear to remain so long without you. So if you will not give me leave, expect me without it some day. And indeed it is very likely that you may for I am quite sick of passing day after day in this hopeless way." Suddenly, she interrupted herself as though her suppressed fears had to erupt. "Pray is Clary with you? . . . it would not in the least surprise me if you have written to her from London and let her know that you are without me that she should have taken some such freak—"

The thought that perhaps he *was* feeling the temptation to go off alone preyed on her mind. Her pregnancy had upset the balance of power in their relationship. Shelley was free to walk off, to have an affair, even to leave her for Claire, as he had left Harriet for her. If he did leave, what could she do but crawl home to her family to give birth to a bastard?

Whether or not Shelley had been contemplating leaving her, he didn't. Instead, he found a house at Bishopsgate, close to Windsor Great Park, near Windsor in the Thames River valley west of London. It was a brick cottage standing alone, with a flower garden. They rented it furnished for a year. Now they had the beauty of the countryside and the Thames flowing nearby. Their friend Thomas Love Peacock lived a few miles away in Marlow, and Hogg, clearly just a friend now, visited from London.

And they had a boat. Boats were Shelley's passion, as mountains were Mary's. "Shelley's favorite taste was boating," Mary wrote years later, "when living near the

Thames, or by the lake of Geneva, much of his life was spent on the water. On the shore of every lake, or stream, or sea, near which he dwelt, he had a boat moored."

They regained health and happiness at Bishopsgate during the pleasant summer of 1815. Among shady trees and boat rides on the Thames, they lived a simple life of work and leisure. Although Mary was pregnant, she refused to lace herself as most women did and wore loose, comfortable clothing. With the help of a maid and a cook, she whisked through her housekeeping, preparing simple meals. They didn't eat meat or drink alcohol and had given up sugar, produced by slave workers, as a political protest.

At the end of August, along with Peacock and Mary's stepbrother, Charles Clairmont, they took a boat trip up the river to Lechlade, stopping on the way at Oxford to see the very rooms where Shelley and Hogg, "the two noted infidels," as Charles called them, had pored like alchemists over the "boundaries of human knowledge." Perhaps an idea sparked in Mary's mind at that point for a story about an "infidel" student, one who worked in secret in a well-known university to create something diabolic.

For months Shelley hadn't been feeling well. He believed he had consumption, as tuberculosis was then called. He often had spasms of intense pain and thought he was dying. A doctor confirmed that he had abscesses on his lungs. Peacock, who blamed Shelley's poor health on his diet of tea, lemonade, and bread and butter, prescribed "three mutton chops, well-peppered."

Shelley obeyed and for whatever reason—peace, serenity, or peppered mutton chops—his health during and after the boat trip improved dramatically. Though he still had bouts of intense pain, every other symptom vanished. No longer sad and irritable, he gained enough energy to work six hours a day.

Mary spent most of her time, as usual, reading and studying. In 1815 alone, she read more than seventy-five books, including the New Testament, Geoffrey Chaucer's *Canterbury Tales,* John Milton's *Paradise Lost* and *Paradise Regained,* Edmund Spenser's *Faerie Queene,* and Homer's *The Iliad,* as well as novels—including the works of Romantic horror writers such as Ann Radcliffe and Matthew "Monk" Lewis—plays, poetry, history, and biography, especially those written by her parents. Shelley was teaching her Latin, and she read books in that language too. Mary didn't just read. She took notes on what she read. She did work equivalent to that required for a graduate degree in comparative literature today.

Shelley, as well as reading, was also writing poetry. A new generation of Romantic poets was rising to replace William Wordsworth and Mary's old friend Samuel Taylor Coleridge, the founders of the English Romantic movement. Chief among these new poets was George Gordon Byron, sixth Baron of Rochdale, who introduced the world to the Romantic hero—dark, brooding, daring, insolent, and tempestuous—in his poetry and in his life. Two other young Romantics who would eventually rise to Byron's level were John Keats, who, dying young, was the subject of *Adonais,* one of Shelley's most beautiful poems, and Percy Bysshe Shelley himself.

Up to now, Shelley had been barely known except as the author of *Queen Mab* and some radical pamphlets. In

September 1815, he began *Alastor: Or the Spirit of Solitude,* his first mature poetic work. In abstract language, it describes the quest of a poet tempted by the evil spirit of solitude and indifferent to human love until too late. Its theme may have been inspired by Shelley's decision to commit himself to Mary. Her fears, earlier that summer, that he was drawing away from her appear to have been well founded. He had perhaps felt attracted to "solitude," but rejected it as leading to the death of the self and had chosen love instead.

Mary, however, wasn't writing, though Shelley wanted her to, urging her, she later said, "to prove myself worthy of my parentage, and enrol myself on the page of fame." On the basis of a superior education, he'd assumed the role of teacher, critic, and judge, though she'd probably learned more under her father's tutoring than Shelley had under the lax university standards of his day. He said that he didn't expect her to produce anything "worth notice," just something that would allow him to judge whether she could do better later on. She wanted to write, but it was difficult under so watchful an eye.

On January 24, 1816, around the time Shelley published *Alastor,* Mary gave birth, this time to a healthy little boy. She named him William after her father, hoping that Godwin would now reconcile with her, as angry parents often do once a grandchild is born. Shelley wrote to Godwin, pointing out that they were "a young family, innocent and benevolent and united," not to be confused with "prostitutes and seducers." But to Mary's great sadness, Godwin continued to shut her out. Mrs. G. raged at Mary, "her greatest enemy in the world," whose fault it was that her hopes for Claire were dashed. Godwin believed that Shelley was evil and that Mary, Claire, and even Fanny had fallen under his spell.

Godwin was again nagging Shelley to pay his debts. Mary felt pulled two ways. She agreed with Shelley that it was difficult to be generous to someone who treated them so badly. Yet, despite everything, she still believed that her father deserved their support. Evidently Shelley did too, for he told Godwin that he regretted not having enough money to give him all he needed "for the comfort and independence which it is so unjust that you should not have already received from society."

The Godwins weren't the only troublesome members of her family. While Mary and Shelley enjoyed their peaceful summer at Bishopsgate, Claire had been dramatizing herself as an outcast in Lynmouth: "day after day I sat companionless upon that unfrequented sea-shore, mentally exclaiming, 'A life of sixteen years is already too much for me to bear.'" In a different mood, she rhapsodized to Fanny over the beauty of her cottage "with jessamine and honeysuckle twining over the window." She was "perfectly happy," she insisted, but felt "anxious to be wise, to be capable of knowing the best, of following resolutely—however painful—what nature and serious thought may prescribe."

Her resolution to be wise didn't last long. By January she was back in London, pursuing a new plan. If Mary could snag herself a handsome poet, why couldn't she? And an even more famous poet—in fact, the most famous poet and writer in Europe—the handsome, wealthy, aristocratic, notorious Lord Byron himself.

Byron—adored by half of Europe for his genius, loathed by the other half for his sins—had a degree of fame that rock stars and film idols of today might envy. After publishing *Childe Harold* in 1812, he became the most fashionable author of his day. For three years, hostesses vied for the honor of having him in their drawing rooms. Women found him irresistible. After a series of love affairs, he married, but a year later his marriage failed. Rumors flew: He'd forced unnatural practices upon his bride; he'd slept with his half-sister. He was hissed at in the House of Lords. Hounded by English morality, he was planning to make his escape.

One day in March, he received a letter from a Miss E. Trefusis. Would he look at the enclosed story and give his opinion? This was nothing new. As a member of the theater committee at Drury Lane Theatre, he was forever getting letters from a "Miss Emma Somebody with a play entitled 'The Bandit of Bohemia.'" But this letter went on to ask a question sure to provoke his interest: "If a woman, whose reputation has as yet remained unstained, if without either guardian or husband to control, she should throw herself on your mercy, if with a beating heart she should confess the love she has borne you many years. . . . Could you betray her, or would you be silent as the grave?" In her attack on Byron, Claire, alias Miss E. Trefusis, had fired the first shot.

His reply was cool, but she persisted, asking to see him alone and with "utmost privacy." He agreed. Claire, now seventeen, was dark-haired, pretty, clever, and known for her beautiful singing voice. She flirted, she chatted, sh sang. Her voice, at least, enchanted Byron. He

"There Be None of Beauty's Daughters," one of his most famous poems, as tribute to the music she made.

But he held back. Claire was neither beautiful nor sophisticated enough for him to take altogether seriously. Besides, although he tumbled actresses and servant girls without a qualm, Claire was of a well-known middle-class family, obviously young and inexperienced despite her bravado.

Claire played what cards she had. She knew the daughter of Mary Wollstonecraft and William Godwin. Would he like to meet her? In April, without telling Mary what her interest in Byron was, Claire brought her stepsister to his London mansion. Mary was favorably impressed. "How mild he is! How gentle! How different from what I expected."

Claire then moved in for the kill. "Have you any objection to the following plan?" she asked him. "On Thursday evening we go out of town together by some stage or mail about the distance of ten or twelve miles. There we shall be free and unknown; we shall return early the next morning. I have arranged everything here so that the slightest suspicion may not be excited."

Byron gave in. "I never loved or pretended to love her," he told a friend, "but a man is a man, and if a girl of eighteen [she was actually younger] comes prancing to you at all hours there is but one way—"

Claire seems to have had the mind of a groupie, believing that if she shared a bed with a famous person, the glamour would rub off. Or else she truly believed that sex with Byron would lead to the kind of relationship Mary had with Shelley. But the stepsisters were dealing with different men. Where Shelley was idealistic, Byron was cynical.

Although she seemed brave and sure of herself, Claire lacked self-esteem. She groveled. "I do not expect you to love me," she said. "I am not worthy of your love." Of "all human evils none can affect me except offending you." On the other hand, she couldn't accept that for him their affair had been about sex and that he grew tired of her. She was supposed to fade away. Instead, she clung. She was acting a part in a play she'd written herself, but the other actor had no intention of following her script. When she found out that he planned to leave for Switzerland in April, she was desperate. Even she didn't have the nerve to go traipsing across the Continent alone in pursuit of her reluctant lover.

But Mary and Shelley were also talking of leaving England. Their idyll in Bishopsgate was at an end. Harassed by Godwin for money, shunned by the proper English for their "immorality," *Alastor* neglected by critics or treated harshly, they were ready to go. Italy was their destination, but Claire persuaded them to head for Switzerland instead. She told Shelley that she could introduce him to Byron—a strong inducement to the still barely known Shelley. Besides, Mary had loved Switzerland since the first time she'd seen it. They easily gave way.

On May 3, 1816, Mary, Shelley, and Claire—along with little William—once again left England's cold, clammy puritanical shores for the sunshine, mountains, and sweet air of the south.

Less than two weeks later, they arrived at Lake Leman and registered at the Hotel d'Angleterre in Secheron near

Geneva, where all well-to-do English people stayed. Byron was expected but had not yet arrived. Forbidden to enter France, he'd been forced to travel the long way around. But it was comfortable traveling. His coach had every amenity—his books, a bed to sleep in, dishes, glasses, and cutlery for meals on the road. John William Polidori, Byron's private physician whom he called Polly Dolly and teased unmercifully, accompanied him and took notes. A publisher was paying him to write a book about Byron.

Late on May 25, Claire came in from sailing on the lake and checked the register. Byron's name was there at last. He had written his age next to it as *1,000*. She wrote him a note: "I am sorry you are grown so old. Indeed I suspected you were 200 from the slowness of your journey. I suppose your venerable age could not bear quicker traveling. . . . I am so happy."

Byron, who didn't bother to answer, spent the next two days house-hunting with Polidori. Claire couldn't catch a glimpse of him. Then on the twenty-seventh, as she walked by the lake with Mary and Shelley, she saw Polidori rowing Byron to shore. She introduced Shelley to Byron as the author of *Queen Mab*. That night, Shelley dined with Byron and Polidori. Claire and Mary stayed home.

The rising young Romantic poet and the established one hit it off at once. They bought a boat together to sail around the lake. Both rented lakeside houses close beside each other in Coligny, a few miles outside Geneva's city gates.

The little community of literary friends intrigued the neighborhood. Among other rumors, it was said that Shelley was sleeping with both sisters. Tourists rented telescopes from the innkeeper at Secheron, hoping to catch glimpses of these scandalous English. If those telescopes were powerful enough, they might often have seen the figure of Claire scurrying up the path and into Byron's ground-floor bedroom late at night.

Mary and Shelley settled down to their usual routine of reading, writing, study, and conversation, punctuated with outings on the lake, on which Mary sometimes brought infant William clasped in her arms. Byron and Shelley often sailed together while Mary sat and talked with Polidori. If the weather was too wet for an evening excursion, they all gathered at the Villa Diodati, the magnificent house Byron had rented, remaining there for the night if the weather was very bad.

"We often sat up in conversation till the morning light," Mary said. "There was never any lack of subjects, and, grave or gay, we were always interested." It was the closest she ever came to going to university. She was having all the fun of college life, without the tests.

TEN

Conceiving Frankenstein

It was on a dreary night of November that I beheld the accomplishment of my toils. With an anxiety that almost amounted to agony, I collected the instruments of life around me, that I might infuse a spark of being into the lifeless thing that lay at my feet. It was already one in the morning; the rain pattered dismally against the panes, and my candle was nearly burnt out, when, by the glimmer of the half-extinguished light, I saw the dull yellow eye of the creature open; it breathed hard, and a convulsive motion agitated its limbs.

—from *Frankenstein* by Mary Shelley

The thunderous weather that had heralded Mary Godwin's birth also heralded the birth of her most famous creation. A year earlier, in 1815, Mount Tambora in Indonesia had erupted, spewing enormous clouds of gases into the atmosphere. By the spring of 1816, the gases, settling high into the stratosphere, were reflecting sunlight away from Earth and back into space. The result was no sun, torrents of rain and hail, and the coldest summer ever recorded. Astrologers predicted the end of the world.

All over Europe, the cold and wet caused the harvest to fail, resulting in the worst food shortages of the century. Mary received a letter from her sister Fanny complaining of the dreariness of an England shrouded in constant cold and rain.

In Switzerland, the elements had raged for weeks. Through night after night of "almost perpetual rain," Mary exulted in thunderstorms "grander and more terrific than I have ever seen before," as she watched lightning flash and knife among the pine-covered mountaintops in the skies above Lake Leman.

"One night," she wrote to Fanny, "we *enjoyed* a finer storm than I had ever before beheld. The lake was lit up— the pines on Jura made visible, and all the scene illuminated for an instant, when a pitchy blackness succeeded, and the thunder came in frightful bursts over our heads amid the darkness."

As with many good stories, the story of *Frankenstein's* conception begins on a dark and stormy night: June 16, 1816. As usual Mary, Shelley, Claire, Byron, and Polidori were gathered together in the elegant drawing room of the Villa Diodati. Light glittered from the chandeliers, warmth rose from a glowing fire, and the reflected splendor of high ceilings and Louis XV furniture gleamed from the round mirror above the mantelpiece.

Byron had a treat for his guests that night, a book of old ghost stories. *Fantasmagoriana,* it was called, *A Collection of the Histories of Apparitions, Spectres, Ghosts, etc.* What could be more perfect than spooky stories for a stormy night? Byron opened the book and began to read.

Shelley, enraptured as always by tales of ghosts and graves, widened his staring blue eyes as he listened. Polidori stretched out on the sofa, nursing a sore ankle and sulking from one of Byron's taunts, but listening too. Claire sat back in the shadows cast by candles and flickering firelight, her eyes fixed on Byron as he read.

Like the others, Mary was caught up in Byron's masterful reading of the tales, shivering at stories like the one about a horrified bridegroom who clasped the ghost of his deserted lover to his breast and the one about a ghostly ancestor who gave his young descendents the kiss of death.

Outside the French windows that opened onto the verandah, Mary could hear the dark storm rage. Rain beat down on Lake Leman and on the towers and turrets of Geneva, poured down on the cottages and mansions tucked here and there on the surrounding hillsides, and streamed down the sides of the little stone cottage nestled within a vineyard—the Maison Chapuis—that Mary had shared with Shelley and Claire for the past few weeks. Five-month-old William, her darling Willman, her Willmouse, was tucked up there now fast asleep under the care of his Swiss nurse.

Byron slammed the book shut. "We will each write a ghost story." They were talented young people. Why not?

The three men had no problem coming up with ideas. Byron decided to write about a vampire, and Shelley about a ghostly experience he'd had growing up. Polidori had an idea for a story about "a skull-headed lady" who was "punished for peeping through a keyhole." Mary laughed. She thought his idea was silly.

Poor Polidori. Avid to be a writer, he was a mere weed in this hotbed of literary genius. The friendship between Shelley and Byron, who teased Polidori without mercy, had put his nose out of joint. A few nights earlier, he'd read aloud a play he'd written, "which all," he noted in his diary, "agreed was worth nothing."

Claire may have had a story idea, too. As her journals and letters show, she was a good writer, sharp-tongued and witty, a bit cynical—always willing to see the darker side of life. She did, years later, try to publish a book she'd once written. It may have been *The Idiot,* the novel she'd started two years earlier in France. It may have been the story she sent to Byron. It may have been a ghost story she started that night. In any case, it wasn't published and the manuscript has disappeared.

Of them all, nineteen-year-old Mary took Byron's challenge most seriously. Here was a chance to prove herself. Although it was exciting to spend night after night of rain and storm in a glamorous villa with two of the most talented and romantic men in Europe, it was frustrating too. As electric currents ignited the skies above the lake, undercurrents as flashing and dangerous as electricity sparked around the aristocratic Lord Byron. Older, wealthier, and more famous than the rest, Byron was admired by Shelley, envied by Polidori, and idolized by Claire.

Mary feared him. His overwhelming personality intimidated her. She knew that she didn't fit his ideas of what a woman should be, being neither witty, flirtatious, and in-dependent, nor soft, clinging, and sweet. As his friend Edward John Trelawny once observed, "He treated women as things devoid of soul or sense; he would not eat, pray, walk, nor talk with them." A bit of an exaggera-tion, but not by much.

Like Polidori, Mary felt shunted aside by the Shelley-Byron friendship. Wasn't she Shelley's soulmate? Yet now, while she was tied down with the cares of a household and a baby, he was off sailing with Byron every day. Might Shelley not pick up some of Byron's attitudes?

Byron was working on the third part of *Childe Harold.* Shelley had just completed *Alastor.* Except for five-month-old William, Mary had produced nothing. During the nightly discussions, Byron and Shelley did most of the talking. She sat in the shadows with Claire, taking it all in. Writing a story would show them she was not a Polidori, to be ignored by the real writers in the group, not a Claire, focused on her sexual life, but a true daugh-ter of Godwin and Wollstonecraft.

Mary struggled to come up with an idea for a story as good as those Byron had read, one "which would speak to the mysterious fears of our nature and awaken thrilling horror—one to make the reader dread to look round, to curdle the blood, and quicken the beatings of the heart." But as often happens, wanting desperately to succeed, she couldn't think of a thing. That night and for several nights afterward, she lay awake pondering, discarding one idea, then another. None seemed just right.

Every morning, Shelley asked her, "Have you thought of a story?" and every morning she had to say no. Shelley, whose talents were more suited to poetry, had given up on his own story idea, but he wanted her to succeed.

Every evening, as the rain continued, Mary sat in the shadows at Villa Diodati, listening to Shelley and Byron. One night, talking of the marvels and possibilities of new scientific discoveries, they discussed whether scientists would ever discover the principle of life. The subject was in the air. Scientists debated it in lecture halls and magazine articles. Materialists said that life consisted of body parts and chemicals. Period. Vitalists claimed that something more, something invisible, was needed for inanimate matter to come alive.

Perhaps the answer lay in galvanism. In 1791, an Italian scientist named Luigi Galvani had experimented on the muscles of dissected frogs. When he put two pieces of metal in contact with each other and touched them to a muscle, the muscle twitched. Galvani correctly assumed that an electric current caused the twitching.

Like cloning today, such advances in science exercised people's imaginations, making them wonder *What if?* Would it ever be possible to use an electric current to bring a dead body to life? Byron and Shelley talked it over until after midnight.

Mary finally went to bed, her brain teeming with ideas. As she lay down, moonlight filtered in through closed shutters. All that she had heard that night flitted through her mind. Exhausted, she drifted into a state between waking and sleep. Vivid images pressed against closed eyelids. A vision formed.

A creature, a huge, inanimate thing in the shape of a man, stretched out upon a table. A young scientist kneeling beside it hushed, waiting. Will his experiment work? Suddenly the thing jerks a muscle. Opens an eye.

Other images followed. *The thing's creator flees. Falls asleep. Wakes up. The thing is at his bedside, staring down at him with watery, yellow eyes.*

Mary shuddered, forced her eyes open, sat up. Grotesque, that a dead thing should live! Like Byron and Shelley, she'd been tantalized by the idea of animating lifeless matter. But some part of her mind, realizing what the two men had not, had brought the poets' airy speculations to earth, grounded them in reality, and envisioned the horror that would result if they came true.

As she tried to calm herself, she thought once again of the ghost story she wanted to write. If only she could think of an idea that would frighten others as she had just frightened herself. And of course she immediately realized she had. When morning came, she picked up her pen and began.

It was on a dreary night of November. . . .

How does a novelist's mind work? Like Mary's hero Victor Frankenstein, the young scientist who cobbled his monster together out of parts of corpses, a novelist gathers bits and pieces from here and there, arranges them into a definite shape, then uses her genius to spark them into life.

In late July, for example, Mary and Shelley took a week's trip to nearby Chamounix and climbed up into the magnificent ice field, the Mer de Glace, or Sea of Ice, that covers the mountain for miles. What a wonderful landscape for the second meeting of the monster and his creator. And down it went upon the page.

Like many writers, Mary had a highly developed visual imagination. She saw images in her mind, then made stories out of them, a talent she had developed as she dreamed among the tombstones in St. Pancras churchyard and in the mountains near Dundee.

Mary once said that creation comes not from nothingness, but from chaos, a confusing whirl of material. Imagination "can give form to dark, shapeless substances but cannot bring into being the substance itself." She opened herself up to the chaos of her unconscious, to the shifting jumble of thoughts and impressions that lodged there. Then she selected and shaped, ruthlessly rejecting whatever didn't fit the image in her mind.

At first, Mary planned to write *Frankenstein* as a short story. But as she worked on it, other possibilities came to her and she enlarged it into a novel. *Frankenstein* is Mary's monster. She constructed it out of bits and pieces, just as her hero Victor constructed his. And some of her bits and pieces were as grisly as Victor's.

Or—another image—like an old-fashioned cook, a novelist keeps a stockpot going on the stove, throws in leftovers and fresh meats, slow-simmers and stirs it, then strains the broth until only the rich essence of all the ingredients remains.

Books read, tales heard, life lived—all go into the pot. *A white stone grave. A motherless child. A beloved father turning his back. A young university student concocting wild experiments. Dreams of rekindling life in an infant dead in its cradle.*

The myth of Prometheus, who made man in defiance of the gods and was punished with an eternity of anguish. Milton's story in *Paradise Lost* of creatures who turn away from the god that made them. Coleridge's ancient mariner, doomed to wander the world. Mountains, ghost stories, galvanism, the plight of the poor.

As Mary worked on her story over the next year, new events would occur, new images sink into her brain.

The dead body of a woman in a lonely room in a Welsh inn. A scrap of paper bearing a fragment of a poem, a sketch of a grave, and the words, "It is not my fault."

Another dead woman, this one fished cold and dripping from a lake in a London park—and again the cry, "I am not to blame."

Two children dragged through a court case, then abandoned.

All grisly bits and pieces for the *Frankenstein* pot.

ELEVEN

Fanny and Harriet

Friend, had I known thy secret grief

Her voice did quiver as we parted,
Yet knew I not that heart was broken
From which it came, and I departed
Heeding not the word then spoken.
Misery—O misery,
This world is all too wide for thee.

—from a poem by
Percy Bysshe Shelley, 1817

Claire was pregnant. Byron and Shelley, who had loved the idea of a man creating a human being without the help of a woman, found a woman who created a child without the legal protection of a man embarrassing and vexing. They sat up nights with Claire, devising a plan that would avoid further scandal and provide for the baby's future. Because Byron had no intention of continuing the relationship, they decided that Claire would return to England with Mary and Shelley and live in seclusion until her baby was born. When it was old enough, it would be shipped off to Byron.

They arrived back in England in the fall of 1816. Because they didn't want the Godwins to know of Claire's pregnancy, they couldn't go to London so they rented lodgings in the city of Bath. Shelley went to London to attend to business. Mary quickly resumed work on *Frankenstein,* always easier when he was out of the house. Shelley once spoke of *Frankenstein* as "the fruits of my absence."

In abandoning England for Switzerland, Mary, Shelley, and Claire had left a good deal of misery in their wake. While they were sailing on Lake Leman, buoyed up by good companions and bright futures, others were sinking at home, borne down by loneliness and need. Fanny, Mary's half-sister, and Harriet, Shelley's deserted wife, saw no bright futures before them, only a continuation of the misery they already endured.

Poor, wretched Fanny Imlay Godwin! "A very plain girl and odd in her manners and opinions," someone who knew her said, "but upright and generous," adding, "She was pitied and respected."

Since the summer when Charles Clairmont had left London, Fanny had been alone with Mr. and Mrs. Godwin. Twenty-two years old, with no job and little chance of marrying, she depended for money and affection on two financially burdened people who didn't let her forget that she wasn't their biological child. She had tried to write cheerful letters to Mary, but her misery leaked through, "the dreadful state of mind I generally labour under and which I in vain endeavor to get rid of."

Fanny took Godwin at his own valuation. She hero-worshipped him as much as Mary did—perhaps more, with that peculiar intensity of the less-favored child—and was blind to his faults. Godwin, who still didn't write to Shelley or Mary, used Fanny as his go-between. On October 4, she wrote asking them to send him money. "You know he cannot write when pecuniary circumstances overwhelm him; you know that it is of the utmost consequence, for his own and the world's sake, that he should finish his novel; and is it not yours and Shelley's duty to consider these things, and to endeavor to prevent, as far as lies in your power, giving him unnecessary pain and anxiety?"

Mary read the letter and tossed it aside. "Stupid letter from Fanny," she said. Life in Bath, even with a pregnant Claire close by, was too pleasant to let grumbles and mumbles from Skinner Street upset her. Working on her novel fired her imagination. Free to indulge her delight in manufacturing dreams and visions, she grew whimsical. One day she stuck her head through the door from the garden and beckoned to Shelley. "Come and look. Here's a cat eating roses. She'll turn into a woman. When beasts eat these roses they turn into men and women."

Perhaps because she lacked charm and imagination herself, Fanny admired them in Mary. Mrs. Godwin, who resented having been forsaken by her own daughter, mocked Fanny for it, telling her she was Mary's "laughing-stock and the constant beacon" of her satire. Yet Fanny tried to be fair to Mrs. G., even called her Mamma although she was merely her stepfather's wife, and defended her when Mary accused her of spreading malicious rumors.

"Mamma and I are not great friends—but I'm always alive to her virtues." True, Mrs. G. talked against Mary and Shelley in private, and her remarks might not always be "the most just or the most amiable—but they are always confined to myself and Papa."

Once, Fanny knew, in the few short years while her mother was alive, she too had been loved. When she ran into an old friend of Mary Wollstonecraft's, she listened with delight to his recollections of her goodness, generosity, and courage. "I have determined never to live to be a disgrace to *such a mother*," she said.

Needing to feel attached somewhere, Fanny poured her love onto Mary and Shelley. With their beauty, talent, and exciting friends, they represented all that was glamorous and free. Fanny read all of Byron's poems and besieged Mary with questions. What did he look like? Was he as wicked as people said? She tried to live through them. "Kiss Dear William for me—I sometimes consider him as my child and look forward to the time of my old age and his manhood." In London, where Shelley saw and talked to Fanny, his kind, friendly manner may have sparked hopes he couldn't fulfill.

Painfully aware of the Godwins' lack of money, Fanny felt herself a burden, especially because Mrs. G. complained even of the money she spent on postage. She needed a job, but jobs for impoverished gentlewomen were as few and far between as they had been for her mother a generation earlier.

Her one hope was to work as a governess or teacher. Her aunts Everina and Eliza, Mary Wollstonecraft's sisters, ran a school in Dublin, Ireland. They had talked of coming to London to discuss whether to hire Fanny to teach. It wasn't an exciting prospect—Aunt Everina was known for her harshness. But she would be useful, earning her own money. During the summer of 1816, Fanny awaited their arrival, "when my future fate will be decided."

By late summer, the aunts had come—and gone. Apparently they made no offer, yet Fanny didn't seem upset, perhaps because she cherished a new dream. Mary and Shelley were no longer on the Continent but right here in England. Why shouldn't she live with them? She wouldn't mind living on the sidelines of their life, being the maiden aunt, bestowing kisses on little William and sisterly advice on Shelley, easing Mary's burdens where she could.

It was an impossible dream. In the eyes of the world, she was a respectable young woman; Mary was a ruined woman living in sin with a married man and her illegitimate child. Although Mary was willing to brave the world's censure for herself, she couldn't let Fanny throw away her good name.

Fanny didn't see it that way. She told the Godwins she was going to Wales to visit some Wollstonecraft relatives. Bath was on the way. She wrote to Mary to let her know she was coming.

Tuesday morning, October 8, Fanny dressed carefully. Over stays marked *M.W.* that had belonged to her mother, she put on a blue-striped skirt with a white bodice, a brown pelisse lined with white silk and trimmed with light-brown fur, and a hat to match. She wore a small

French gold watch Mary and Shelley had bought her. In her reticule, she placed a red silk pocket handkerchief, a brownberry necklace, and a small leather clasped purse.

Her coach, which arrived in Bath the next morning, had a stop of several hours before continuing on to Bristol for the next leg of the journey. Perhaps she wouldn't have to go on at all. Perhaps she could talk to Shelley or Mary or both and explain her situation. When they saw how miserable she was, they would make an offer and she could stay.

If that was her plan, she was disappointed. She probably did visit with Mary and Shelley. But when the afternoon coach set off for Bristol, Fanny was on it. At Bristol, she wrote two letters, one to Godwin, one to Mary and Shelley. To Godwin, she wrote, "I depart immediately to the spot from which I hope never to remove"; to Mary and Shelley, "By the time you read this, I will be dead."

Fanny continued her journey to Swansea in Wales, arriving by evening at an inn, the Mackworth Arms, where she had tea. She went to her room, telling the chambermaid she was very tired and would take care of the candle herself. She wrote a note:

> I have long determined that the best thing I could do was to put an end to the existence of a being whose birth was unfortunate, and whose life has only been a series of pain to those persons who have hurt their health in endeavoring to promote her welfare. Perhaps to hear of my death will give you pain, but you will soon have the blessing of forgetting that such a creature ever existed as. . . .

She signed her name, then tore off her signature and burned it. She took a bottle of laudanum from her reticule, drank it down, and died.

Mary and Shelley received her note that same night. Shelley read it, thrust his hand in his hair, and jumped up. "I must be off," he said, ordered a post-chaise, and was gone. By Friday, he'd traced Fanny to Swansea. In a newspaper account he read there, he discovered he'd arrived too late.

When Godwin found out, his response was to keep the news covered up. "Go not to Swansea," he wrote to Shelley,

> disturb not the silent dead; do nothing to destroy the obscurity she so much desired that now rests upon the event. It was, as I said, her last wish; it was the motive that led her from London to Bristol and from Bristol to Swansea. . . .
>
> . . . do not expose us to those idle questions, which to a mind in anguish is one of the severest of all trials. . . . What I have most of all in horror is the public papers. . . .

He'd tell people she'd "gone to Ireland with her aunt." And so Fanny's unidentified body was buried in an unmarked grave because Godwin wished to shield her reputation and his own. Which carried the greater weight, only he could know. Even in August of 1817, Charles Clairmont still didn't know the truth. Godwin placed blame for the suicide on Shelley and Mary. "From the fatal day of Mary's elopement, Fanny's mind had been unsettled, her duty kept her with us: but I am afraid her affections were with them."

Shelley was disturbed by her death, suggesting he felt himself responsible, perhaps for encouraging unrealistic hopes. He wrote a poem about Fanny which began, "Friend, had I known thy secret grief." On the back of the page he sketched a picture of a grave and wrote underneath, "These cannot be forgotten. It is not my fault—it is not to be alluded to."

Mary, also deeply distressed, went on writing. By November 20, she was ready to start the second volume of *Frankenstein*, which opens with the monster telling his own story. Homely, unloved Fanny, whose hopes of finding a home were so cruelly dashed, was on her mind. Transformed by Mary's imagination, Fanny lived again in the lonely creature abandoned by the man who gave him life, repulsed by everyone who saw him, cheated of the love he hoped to gain. By December 5, she'd finished chapter four in which the monster hopes the family he's been secretly watching will take him in. She told Shelley, "I think you will like it."

Calamity followed calamity. Ten days later, when Mary was about halfway through her novel, news came that Shelley's wife, Harriet, had killed herself. Her drowned pregnant body had been taken from the Serpentine, a small lake in London's Hyde Park.

Up to September 9, Harriet had lived at her parents' house. She had secretly taken a lover, an army officer who was ordered abroad. His letters didn't reach her, so she thought he had abandoned her, just as Shelley had. When she told her sister Eliza she was pregnant, Eliza rented a room for her at No. 7 Elizabeth Street in Chelsea under the name Harriet Smith. To avoid scandal, Eliza told the landlords that Harriet had been her personal servant, a married woman whose husband had been sent abroad. She told their parents that Harriet was visiting friends in the country for a few weeks.

Harriet couldn't endure the loneliness and shame. "I don't think I am made to inspire love," she told Eliza, "and you know my husband abandoned me." On November 9, a dark, rainy day, she drowned herself. As no one claimed her body, it was taken to St. George's workhouse and buried at the expense of the parish in burial grounds opposite Hyde Park.

Shelley's version of the story seems to have sprung from his imagination—that she was driven from her father's house and "descended the steps of prostitution until she lived with a groom of the name of Smith, who deserting her, she killed herself." Somehow, it was all Eliza's fault—she had as good as murdered her sister to inherit her father's fortune. Everyone—that is, all his friends—agreed that *he* was not in the least to blame.

Harriet left a letter for Eliza. "Too wretched to exert myself, lowered in the opinion of everyone, why should I drag on a miserable existence? embittered by past recollections and not one ray of hope to rest on for the future." In those days, in the eyes of the law, children belonged to their father. Harriet expected that Shelley would want their two-year-old son Charles to live with him. But she prayed he would grant her "last request to let Ianthe remain with you [Eliza] always. Dear lovely child, with you she will enjoy much happiness, with him none."

There is no evidence that Shelley ever tried to visit Ianthe and Charles before Harriet's death or that he helped them in any way or had any particular feeling for them, except that Mary later said he did. William seems to have been the only child of his of whom he was genuinely fond, as long as he didn't come too close. In December 1816, Mary wrote:

> The blue eyes of your sweet boy are staring at me while I write this. He is a dear child and you love him tenderly, although I fancy your affection will increase when he has a nursery to himself and only comes to you dressed and in good humour. . . . Tell me shall you be happy to have another little squaller? You will look grave on this, but I do not mean anything. [She was pregnant again, though she didn't yet know it.]

Nevertheless, Shelley raced to London at once to get the children. If the Westbrooks—Harriet's parents and sister—would not surrender them, there would be a court fight. He wrote to Eliza to tell her that she must give up three-year-old Ianthe: "there is no earthly consideration which would induce me to forego the exclusive and entire charge of my child." He didn't want them to stay with Eliza a moment longer, because he feared she'd poison Ianthe's mind against Mary. "Nothing can shake my resolution," he concluded. "The lapse of a few weeks would only render the execution of it more distressing to you. As to Ianthe, a child's sorrows are over in a few hours."

To help his case, on December 30 Mary and Shelley married. Mary regretted that her marriage had come too late to help Fanny. "Poor dear Fanny if she had lived until this moment she would have been saved for my house would then have been a proper asylum for her." It did reconcile Mary with her delighted father. The old radical could be friends with his daughter again now that she was respectable.

On January 3, 1817, Mary went back to work on *Frankenstein.* Nine days later, Claire gave birth to a baby girl, whom she named Alba after Albe, her father's nickname (for *LB,* Lord Byron). Like most new mothers, Claire fell deeply in love with her child, a love poisoned by the knowledge that she would have to give her up. She nursed her, played with her, and sometimes let her sleep in bed with her at night. She delighted in Alba's dark eyes and hair, so like her own. Surrendering her would be painful, especially because she couldn't be sure that Alba's father would love her as she did.

Claire wrote Byron long letters almost daily, describing the baby's charms, predicting how he would enjoy having his little daughter brighten his home. He didn't answer. By now he hated his child's mother. His enthusiasm for Alba was decidedly lukewarm.

Meanwhile, the Westbrooks went to court. The trial lasted almost two months, from January 24 to March 17, 1817. Shelley's marriage didn't help. The forces of the conventional world exerted their power. He was a self-proclaimed atheist, an adulterer who had deserted his wife and children. The Lord Chancellor declared him unfit to have his children because of his immoral principles and conduct. In fact, he was lucky not to be sent to prison and possibly lose little William too.

The children's grandparents and aunt didn't get them either. As their mother's relations, they had no rights; besides, the judge thought the Westbrooks and Eliza "too illiterate and vulgar" to raise the children properly. Instead, the court placed them in the care of a clergyman, a Dr. Hume, and his family. Although Shelley was given monthly visiting rights, there is no evidence that he ever saw Ianthe and Charles again.

In short, Byron and Shelley, whose blithe talk of using science to create life had inspired Mary's story, failed to properly care for the lives they'd created the conventional way. The events Mary witnessed during the year of *Frankenstein*'s creation—the suicides of two lonely and rejected young women, children treated like pawns—gave her book a powerful theme: the need to take responsibility for our actions, especially toward the beings we create.

TWELVE

The Monster and His Maker

Did I request thee, Maker, from my clay
To mould me Man, did I solicit thee
From darkness to promote me?

—from *Paradise Lost* by John Milton

Mary and Shelley had lived in lodgings ever since their return to England. Now they longed for something more homelike, a place of their own that would give them a sense of permanency. On March 18, 1817, they took a twenty-one-year lease on Albion House in Marlow and settled in with little William, Claire, and Alba. They had a garden, four acres of land, and plenty of bedrooms for guests. Godwin visited them in April, followed by their new friends Leigh and Marianne Hunt and their four children. An admirer and promoter of Shelley's poetry, Leigh Hunt was the editor of *The Examiner,* a political and cultural journal. Marianne became Mary's first close woman friend.

Mary was busily engaged in finishing *Frankenstein*. She spent a week in mid-April making corrections. Then came the long job of transcribing it neatly to show to a publisher. On May 14, she was able to write in her journal *Finis*—the end. She had strained her stock, finished constructing her monster and his maker out of the bits and pieces of life's chaos. Her "hideous progeny," as she called it, was ready to come into the world.

Making a fair copy was traditionally the job of a writer's wife or mistress, and Mary had often copied Shelley's work for him. Shelley, however, copied only the last thirteen pages of *Frankenstein*. He also edited it and made corrections.

Readers who have difficulty ploughing through some passages of *Frankenstein* can blame Shelley, who, in his words, "paid considerable attention to the correction of such few instances of baldness of style as necessarily occur in the production of a very young writer." For the sake of our taste, he should have left well enough alone.

Here's an example. In reference to Victor Frankenstein's early love of the supernatural, Mary wrote: "The raising of ghosts or devils was also a favorite pursuit . . ."

Shelley's "improved" version reads: "The raising of ghosts or devils was a promise liberally accorded by my favourite authors, the fulfillment of which I most eagerly sought . . ."

Where Mary wrote *have, wish, caused,* Shelley substituted *possess, desire, derived their origin from.* A *painting* became a *representation; smallness* became *minuteness; talked, conversed; what to say, what manner to commence the interview.* Altogether, he made about a thousand changes in

Mary's manuscript. Some were definite improvements, such as correcting errors in fact and grammar. Others caused the creature to appear more monstrous and less human. Probably because Shelley was the model for Victor, he also made the young scientist seem better than he was.

On May 22, Shelley went to London to submit the manuscript to publisher John Murray, who rejected it. Another publisher turned it down too. Then at the end of August it was accepted by the firm of Lackington, Hughes, Harding, Mavor, and Jones.

Shelley saw it through the press, continuing to correct any "baldness of style" he encountered. Soon after giving birth to a daughter, Clara Everina, on September 1, 1817, Mary was correcting proofs. She then went to work turning the journal she and Shelley kept during their elopement into the *History of a Six Weeks' Tour Through a Part of France, Switzerland, Germany, and Holland.* It was published in December. At the end of that month, she held in her hand the bound copies of the three volumes of *Frankenstein.*

In March 1818, *Frankenstein, or, the Modern Prometheus,* made its official—and anonymous—debut. Most reviewers assumed that a man had written it. Because it was dedicated to Godwin, many thought that Shelley was the author, including Britain's most famous and popular novelist, Sir Walter Scott, who praised the novel's "uncommon powers of poetic imagination," "original genius," and "plain and forcible English."

Most reviews were favorable, although a reviewer named John Wilson Croker made fun of the plot's coincidences, calling it "a tissue of horrible and disgusting absurdity." Yet even he had to admit that *Frankenstein* had "vigour of fancy and language" and "passages which appal the mind and make the flesh creep."

Like any novel, *Frankenstein* belongs to a genre and consists of subject, theme, setting, plot, characters, point of view, and emotional force. It is possible to tease out the threads of Mary's experiences, thoughts, fears, and inner conflicts—some conscious, some not—that went into her masterpiece.

The popularity of Gothic art and literature gave Mary a genre. Ever since the 1790s, the public had craved macabre paintings and horror tales. The first popular reading audience gobbled up cheap editions of ghastly and gruesome stories—*The Monk* by Matthew "Monk" Lewis, *The Mysteries of Udolpho* by Ann Radcliffe, and *The Adventures of Caleb Williams* by Mary's father, William Godwin. Mary read them all and relied on them to shape her own Gothic masterpiece.

The popular interest in the new scientific discoveries that had been made since the 1790s—experimental work on electricity, gases, and combustion, and research into nitrous oxide, voltaic batteries, and the elements of chemical composition—gave Mary a subject. Unlike other Gothic novels, *Frankenstein* is based on science, not the supernatural. It goes beyond the Gothic to create a new genre—science fiction.

Frankenstein's setting comes mainly from places where Mary had lived or visited. Victor Frankenstein lives in Geneva, encounters his creature on the Sea of Ice, rows his bride across Lake Leman, and begins constructing his monster's bride in Scotland. Mary's memories of London life, such as the public hangings at Tyburn, Newgate Prison, Charing Cross, and Tower Hill, provided the gory details.

Hangings were performed every six weeks at Tyburn. At Newgate an average of ten to fifteen criminals were executed at a time. Afterward, the corpses were publicly displayed. Sometimes, the bowels were removed, the head shaved, and the corpse dipped in tar before it went on display. A notorious criminal's corpse might be hung in irons at the site of the original crime.

"Resurrection men," who dug up new graves and sold the bodies to surgeons, were always on the lookout for corpses in good condition. The bodies of giants were particularly popular because they were easier for doctors to work with. Grave robbers hired corpse watchers to let them know when a giant died. No doubt this is how Victor Frankenstein was able to get the oversized body parts he used for his monster.

Many of *Frankenstein*'s themes came from Mary's wide reading. The myth of Prometheus, Jean Jacques Rousseau's *Émile, The Rime of the Ancient Mariner, The Adventures of Caleb Williams*—all sparked her own ideas about creation, the growth of the mind, justice, and sin.

Like her mother, Mary explored feminist themes too. The novel makes us wonder why Victor Frankenstein tries so hard to create life outside a woman's body, why he bothers to do so badly what women already do so well. Perhaps because he's envious and wants the credit of being both mother and father. "A new species would bless me as its creator and source," Victor says. "No father could claim the gratitude of his child so completely as I should deserve theirs." If Victor's plan succeeded, women could become superfluous. Mary also implies that men might muck up the job of reproduction by refusing to take care of what they create.

Mary worked the plot out herself. *Frankenstein*, constructed like an onion, must be unpeeled skin by skin. The outermost layer tells the story of Walton, an explorer bound for the Arctic. He relates how he rescued a distraught traveler—Victor Frankenstein—in letters he writes to his sister back home. The next layer consists of Victor's account of how he built a living being from body parts, then fled in horror from what he had made, until the monster tracks him down. At the core of the novel is the abandoned monster's tale of how he gained knowledge and became an outcast. The novel returns to Victor's point of view as he agrees to create a companion for the monster, then reneges on his promise with terrible consequences. Finally, *Frankenstein* ends as it began, with Walton, who witnesses the end of monster and man.

Mary based her characters on herself and the people she knew and loved. Her monster owes his feelings and situation to her feelings about the fates of Fanny and Harriet, as well as about herself. Like Mary, the monster is motherless, rejected by its father, self-educated, a good student, kind (at least at first), a close observer, and in need of at least one loving companion.

Victor Frankenstein is modeled on Shelley, who as a young boy often called himself Victor. It was the name he used as author of his first published work, the poems he wrote with his sister Elizabeth. Elizabeth was Shelley's closest childhood companion, just as Victor Frankenstein's adopted sister (and fiancée), Elizabeth, is his.

Victor and Shelley share similar traits. Both are high-spirited, passionate, gifted from their earliest days, interested in science, obsessively enthusiastic about current projects, spoiled by their mother and sisters, persuasive, emotionally unstable, reluctant to marry, laudanum users, and apt to say one thing and do another. Victor's relationships with his teachers and father resemble Shelley's with his favorite teachers and Godwin.

Mary uses multiple points of view—Walton's, Victor's, the monster's—to tell her story, suggesting that no one person's perspective is reliable. The story-within-a-story-within-a-story form reveals how difficult it can be to find the truth. Each storyteller has a different view of Victor Frankenstein. And because Victor is closely based on Shelley, they also reveal Mary's conflicted attitudes toward him.

Walton admires Victor Frankenstein tremendously, seeing him as a kindred spirit driven by ambition to explore the unknown. His idealized view of Victor as a tragic hero and near-saint reveals the way Mary perceived Shelley when she first fell in love and how she wanted to go on seeing him.

Victor's view of himself is more modest. He at least admits to making errors, even though he never really blames himself. After telling Walton his story, he says, "During these last days I have been occupied in examining my past conduct; nor do I find it blameable." Despite his responsibility to the creature he created, Victor concludes that he had more responsibility for his fellow human beings, and therefore rightfully refused to make the monster a mate. *He's evil, not me,* is his position, forgetting that by allowing his ugly, ignorant, but powerful creation to roam the world unprotected and uninstructed, he was responsible for turning a goodhearted creature into a fiend.

The monster's view of Victor is the harshest. He sees him as the real monster, a cruel egotist with no thought for the consequences of his actions. This view suggests Mary's own unacknowledged judgment of the husband whom she loved but whose irresponsibility could be hard to bear or forgive. Like her father, Shelley was an idealist, distancing himself from reality and from the affects of his deeds, apt to think up marvelous schemes without thinking them through.

Mary knew that Shelley didn't like to deal with life's realities, its conflicts and tensions, as she was forced to do. He reached for the ideal without noticing the mess he was making in the real world. Even in his writing, "He loved to idealize reality," she later wrote, "taking more delight in the abstract and the ideal, than in the special and the tangible." She said he had "shrunk instinctively from portraying human passion, with its mixture of good and evil, of disappointment and disquiet. Such opened again the wounds of his own heart; and he loved to shelter himself rather in the airiest flights of fancy, forgetting love and hate, and regret and lost hope, in such imaginations as borrowed their hues from sunrise or sunset."

Even in his own account of himself, Victor Frankenstein can unwittingly make himself ridiculous. While going on about beauty, he never seems to notice that he is dabbling in the gruesome. Full of high ideals and lofty language, he digs about in graveyards for corpses, sawing them up and patching them together like some demented child, his head so high in the clouds that he doesn't realize he's wallowing in muck and gore.

Mary's fear of death and her grief at the loss of those she loved give the novel its power. Once she had dreamed that she could rub life back into her dead baby. In *Frankenstein,* she has Victor say, "I thought that if I could bestow animation upon lifeless matter, I might in process of time . . . renew life where death had apparently devoted the body to corruption."

She has Victor dream that his fiancée turned into the corpse of his mother. Did Mary ever have a similar dream? Did she wish, or perhaps fear, to resurrect her mother, that body that lay rotting in the grave she had sat beside day after day? We want the dead to live. At the same time, as stories of ghosts, vampires, and zombies tell us, we want them to stay dead. Victor brought his monster to life then thrust him away in disgust.

For all of us, the fascination with horror in books and movies is an attempt to deal with our fear of death. Mary even has the monster kill a little boy named William, the same name as her own little boy, almost as a charm to keep him safe. (On the other hand, her young half-brother was also named William. Perhaps some half-conscious childhood memory of jealousy toward her stepmother's son resurfaced in her novel. Of course, no well-bred young girl would want to kill a little boy. Only a monster would do that.)

But in life, unlike fiction, Mary had no power over death. The deaths of her mother, her newborn baby girl, Fanny, Harriet—they had been difficult enough to endure. Soon she was to experience deaths that would drive her to the outer reaches of despair.

THIRTEEN

Dead Children

My dearest Mary, wherefore hast thou gone,
And left me in this dreary world alone?
Thy form is here indeed—a lovely one—
But thou art fled, gone down a dreary road.

—from *Posthumous Poems*
of Percy Bysshe Shelley

. . . my cold neglect, averted eyes
That blindly crushed thy heart's fond sacrifice:
My heart was all thine own—but yet a shell
Closed in its core, which seemed impenetrable. . . .

—from "The Choice" by Mary Shelley

By June 1818, when the reviews of *Frankenstein* reached them, Mary and Shelley were in Bagni di Lucca, Italy. They had left England in March, the same month *Frankenstein* was published. Irked that Shelley was considered the author of her book, Mary wrote to Scott

133

and confessed. Soon the news was out. The daughter of Godwin and Wollstonecraft was a recognized author—at age twenty.

Shelley, although still comparatively unknown—Scott seemed to know of him only as Godwin's son-in-law—had also been working steadily. During their peaceful time at Marlow, he had completed a long poem called *The Revolt of Islam,* which he prefaced with a beautiful dedication to his wife:

So now my summer task is ended, Mary,
    And I return to thee, mine own heart's home;
As to his Queen some victor Knight of Faery,
    Earning bright spoils for her enchanted dome;
    Nor thou disdain, that ere my fame become
A star among the stars of mortal night,
    If it indeed may cleave its natal gloom,
Its doubtful promise thus I would unite
    With thy beloved name, thou Child of love and light.

Claire meanwhile had been growing more attached to her child. Mary saw how much she hated the thought of parting with Alba. "Claire although she in a blind kind of manner sees the necessity of it, does not wish her to go and will instinctively place all kinds of difficulties in the way." But Shelley convinced her it was necessary.

It took Byron a long time to agree to accept his daughter into his home, and perhaps his reluctance should have been a warning. Now totally repulsed by Claire, he never answered her frequent long, begging letters, which he said read like bad German novels. He agreed to take Alba on the condition that Claire never see her again. Shelley convinced him to soften his terms, saying he'd get a reputation for cruelty if he ignored a mother's claims.

So in March they all set out for Italy—Mary, Shelley, Claire, two-year-old William, fourteen-month-old Alba, and six-month-old Clara Everina—to improve Shelley's health, to get away from his creditors, and to deliver Alba to Byron. Mary was delighted to be back in warm and sunny southern Europe. "The sun shines bright," she wrote to their friends Leigh and Marianne Hunt, "and it is a kind of Paradise which we have arrived at through the valley of the shadow of death."

By "shadow of death" she meant the actual dangers of their journey, but the phrase was also symbolically true. Fanny and Harriet's deaths were behind them. They had a new baby—a little sister for their beloved Willmouse— and two completed major works. Once Alba was safely with her father, they could relax.

At Bagni di Lucca they read, talked, wrote letters, and went to operas and plays. Shelley bathed in a mountain spring. He and Mary rode horseback in the evenings— alone once Claire fell from a horse and gave it up. Shelley translated Plato. Mary researched her next novel, *Valperga.* She also got to know Maria Gisborne, who, if things had turned out differently, might have been her stepmother. She was one of the women Godwin had proposed to after his first wife's death. She and Mary now became close friends.

In April, Alba, her name changed to Allegra at Byron's order, went with her nurse to Venice to live with her father. In her letters, Claire had painted pretty pictures of Byron's "little darling" running about his house and sitting on his lap. Unfortunately, Allegra looked too much like Claire, and Byron turned his head away in disgust whenever she entered the room.

In August, Claire heard that Byron had foisted the child off on another couple, the Hoppners. Claire was beside herself. Was this why she had given up her child—to be raised by strangers? She insisted on going to Venice at once. Because he couldn't stop her, Shelley went along to keep her in check.

Ten days later, Mary got a letter from Shelley. Claire was with her child. But the Hoppners said Byron had such a horror of Claire that he'd take the child and leave Venice if he knew she was there. Shelley falsely assured him that Mary and the children were close by. Byron agreed to let Allegra stay with them and Claire at a nearby villa for a visit.

Now Shelley feared that if Byron found out he'd lied, he'd change his mind. So Mary must come at once "and scold me if I have done wrong and kiss me if I have done right—for I am sure I do not know which—and it is only the event that can show."

Mary spent August 30, her twenty-first birthday, packing their belongings for the long journey across the Apennine Mountains from the west coast of Italy to the east. The weather was hot, and little Clara, who turned a year old on the trip, was not well. Unsanitary conditions along the way had caused her to develop dysentery, a known baby killer. Constant diarrhea left her dehydrated.

Mary arrived at the villa in Este, a town near Venice, on September 5. The hurried journey had been pointless. Byron had already found out that she wasn't there and hadn't seemed to mind. She called in two different doctors to look at Clara, who grew steadily thinner and weaker.

Byron recommended a famous doctor in Venice. At three o'clock on the morning of September 24, Mary set out with the sick baby in her arms. She met up with Shelley and they rode a barge up a canal for twenty miles to Venice, Clara twitching convulsively all the way. It was five in the afternoon when they arrived. While Mary stayed at an inn with the now desperately ill baby, Shelley hurried off for the doctor. Another doctor came in first and said there was no hope. Mary watched her baby die.

Grief-stricken, she couldn't bear to attend Clara's burial the next day. But she did tell Shelley to ask Byron, for her sake, to allow Claire to spend another month with her daughter. And Byron, to his credit, agreed.

Godwin wrote that this was the time to practice keeping a stiff upper lip. He told her to remember that "only persons of a very ordinary sort" grieve for long. "We seldom indulge long in depression and mourning except when we think secretly that there is something very refined in it, and that it does us honour."

Eight months later, the Shelleys were staying in Rome when three-year-old William became ill. A doctor treated him for worms and suggested that they leave Rome, which was unhealthy, especially during the warmer months. But before they could leave, William got sick again, probably with cholera or typhoid, highly infectious and dangerous diseases.

Worried sick, Mary and Shelley sat by their boy's bedside, watching him suffer the agonies of a raging fever. "The misery of these hours is beyond calculation," Mary wrote Maria Gisborne. "The hopes of my life are bound up in him." At noon on June 7, 1819, William died. Shelley threw himself on the sofa and wept. Mary was beside herself with grief.

After their son was buried in the Protestant Cemetery in Rome, Mary and Shelley traveled to Leghorn (Livorno). Utterly despondent, Mary wrote to Marianne Hunt: "May you my dear Marianne never know what it is to lose two only and lovely children in one year, to watch their dying moments, and then at last to be left childless and forever miserable."

Shelley wrote and told Godwin that Mary was sunk in unhappiness and asked him to write and console her. Godwin's return letter, urging her to get Shelley to give him money, only added to her misery. In another letter, he told her to pull herself together and not delude herself into thinking that there was anything "fine, and beautiful, and delicate" in grief and depression. He warned that others might pity her at first, but "when they see you fixed in selfishness and ill humour, and regardless of the happiness of everyone else, they will finally cease to love you, and scarcely learn to endure you."

By the end of the summer of 1819, Shelley was writing *The Cenci,* a tragedy about a wicked father, while Mary worked on *Matilda,* a short novel about an incestuous father, never published in her lifetime. In October they moved to Florence, where Mary's fourth and only surviving child, Percy Florence, was born on November 12.

Despite her love for her new baby, Mary grew increasingly depressed, consumed with fears that this child too would be taken from her. In January 1820, they moved to Pisa, where they settled in for the next two years and where Mary sometimes went to church. She began writing her new novel, *Valperga.*

In January 1821, another couple, Edward and Jane Williams, moved to Pisa and became close friends. Perhaps too close. Put off by Mary's withdrawal and bolstered by his belief that love shouldn't be exclusive, Shelley was soon writing love poems to Jane. He also became infatuated with Emilia Viviani, a young woman whose father had locked her up in a convent. He wrote *Epipsychidion* for her, the poem in which he stated his philosophy that love should be shared.

On the surface, the Shelleys' relationship seemed fine, although Mary remained cool and withdrawn, still depressed and sometimes irritable since her children's deaths. Shelley, as always, treated her with gentleness and respect. She was too proud to confront him with accusations or complain to her friends of his attentions toward other women. She wrote, she socialized, and she cared for her child and worried about his health while she waited for her husband's infatuations to pass.

Claire, meanwhile, had her own worries. Early in April 1822, she discovered that Byron had put four-year-old Allegra into a convent in the town of Bagnacavallo. Convinced that the damp stone walls of the convent would make the child ill, Claire planned to kidnap her. She begged Mary and Shelley for their help. No, they said. Impossible. It was a bad idea, they hadn't the money, the risk was too great—anything to talk her out of what seemed a crazy, hysterical plan. Mary humored her. Allegra's health wouldn't suffer because "the towns of Romagna where Bagnacavallo is, enjoy the best air in Italy."

"Considering the affair reasonably," which she obviously thought Claire was not, "A. is well taken care of there, she is in good health, and in all probability will continue so." Besides, enclosed as she was by "high walls and bolted doors," rescuing her was highly unlikely. Even if they succeeded, how could they prevent so rich and powerful a man as Byron from getting her back again? Better to wait. In short, as Shelley added in a postscript, "It seems to me that you have no other resource but time and chance and change."

Mary and Shelley were sensible, but Claire proved to be right. Forced to give up her rescue attempt, she joined the others in Pisa three weeks later. The Shelleys and the Williamses planned to rent a couple of houses for the summer at La Spezia, on the shore of a bay a few miles up the Italian coast. On the morning of April 23, Claire set off house-hunting with the Williamses. While she was gone, Mary received a letter informing her that Allegra had died of typhus three days before.

Mary and Shelley didn't know what to do. They were afraid to tell Claire of her daughter's death while she was anywhere near Byron. She'd surely blame him and might seek revenge. So when Claire returned on the twenty-fifth, Mary and Shelley said nothing. Five days later, after a bustle of packing and moving and more frantic house searching, the Shelleys, the Williamses, and Claire moved into Casa Magni, the only house in La Spezia they could find. It was May 2, almost two weeks after Allegra's death, before Claire was told the news of her poor child whose life had been a mistake from first to last.

FOURTEEN

A Sea-Change

Full fathom five thy father lies;
Of his bones are coral made;
Those are pearls that were his eyes:
Nothing of him that doth fade,
But doth suffer a sea-change,
Into something rich and strange.
Sea-nymphs hourly ring his knell:
Hark! now I hear them,—ding-dong bell.

—from *The Tempest*
by William Shakespeare

The one bright spot during this whole miserable time was Shelley's boat. Four months before Allegra's death, the new year of 1822 had begun with a new friend and a new plan. Edward John Trelawny, a sailor friend of the Williamses, had arrived in Pisa. Six feet tall with a dark "Moorish face" and curly black hair, Trelawny was abrupt but good-natured, full of strange stories of his adventures in the Royal Navy. He "has the rare merit of interesting my imagination," Mary said. "His company is delightful for he excites me to think."

One evening as the two couples sat talking after dinner, Trelawny burst in carrying the model of an American schooner. In no time, the three men decided that they must build a thirty-foot-long boat just like it. Jane and Mary teased them for their boyish excitement. "Our husbands decide without asking our consent," Mary said, laughing, "for to tell you the truth, I hate this boat, though I say nothing."

"So do I," Jane replied, "but speaking would be useless, and only spoil their pleasure."

A friend of Trelawny's named Roberts would build the boat for them. Trelawny and Shelley were soon off to nearby Livorno to look at boats and see exactly what they wanted. Not the American model, they decided. Instead, Trelawny wrote to the builder, "will you lay us down a small beautiful one of about 17 or 18 feet? to be a thorough *Varment* at *pulling* and *sailing!*" When Byron heard their plans, he decided to build a boat too.

Trelawny, who kept them informed of each step in their boat's construction, came in one afternoon in high spirits with reports of its progress. "We must all embark, all live aboard," he caroled, then quoted a line from Shakespeare: "We will all suffer a sea-change." The quote delighted Shelley. *We will all suffer a sea-change* would be the motto of their boat.

Since the beginning of the year, they'd also been waiting for the Hunts to join them. Byron, Shelley, and Leigh Hunt had plans of starting a liberal journal together. When their ship didn't arrive, Mary grew worried. "We wait anxiously for them," she wrote her friend Maria Gisborne, "still more anxiously after having heard the wind whistle, and the distant sea roar." And a few days later, "yet the Hunts are not arrived. The storms have been horrible and universal. At Genoa, forty ships were cast away, and 125 souls lost."

By May 2, when they moved into Casa Magni in La Spezia, the Hunts had still not arrived. Mary hated the house. Located on the seashore, away from any roads, it was so isolated that they had to bring their furniture by boat. A footpath connected it to the town of Lerici, a mile away. Mary and Jane groaned the first time they looked inside. The ground floor had no doors or windows, just arched openings and a mud floor. Stairs led to the "splatchy wall, broken floor, cracked ceiling, and poverty-struck appearance" of the main dining hall and four small bedrooms and the "fury of the waves that in blowing weather lashed its walls." Trelawny said that Edward Williams had to talk the women into agreeing to live there. "We men had looked at the sea and scenery, and would have been satisfied with a tent."

Shelley was in fine spirits. His health was good; he loved the wild setting. But Mary was not well. Pregnant again and still locked in despair over her children's deaths, she felt bad—perhaps guilty—about Allegra's death, which also added to her fears for little Percy. Even the woods, beautiful as they were, made her cry and shudder with dislike. "My only moments of peace," she later said, "were aboard that unhappy boat, when lying down with my head on [Shelley's] knee I shut my eyes and felt the wind."

To add to her depression, upsetting letters arrived from her father. Because of a lawsuit over back rent, he would have to give up the bookstore and move from Skinner Street. He insisted she make Shelley lend him money. Shelley refused and finally forbade his father-in-law to send Mary any more letters while she was in her present unhappy state of mind. Shelley was always gentle with Mary and tried to protect her. But he complained to his friends that he suffered too. Mary didn't feel with him, didn't understand him, perhaps, he admitted, because he kept from her thoughts he believed would pain her.

On June 8 she began to bleed. A week later, at eight o'-clock on a Sunday morning, she miscarried. For seven hours, she bled profusely, fainting and coming to again, close to dying in that isolated spot as they waited for the doctor to reach them. Someone sent for ice, which they knew the doctor would probably want. They fed her sips of brandy and applied compresses soaked in vinegar and cologne to her face to keep her from fainting. The ice came eventually, but still no doctor.

Claire and Jane Williams wanted to wait for his arrival, but Shelley decided to take matters into his own hands. He filled a tub with ice and put Mary in it. The bleeding and fainting stopped. When the doctor at last arrived, he praised Shelley for his prompt action, which had undoubtedly saved her life.

One night a week later, Shelley rushed screaming into Mary's sickroom, terrorized by a nightmare. He'd dreamed that Edward, naked, torn, and bleeding, had come into his room and called out, "Get up, Shelley, the sea is flooding the house and it is all coming down." In his dream, he'd looked out on the terrace and seen the sea pouring in. Then the dream changed and he saw himself strangling Mary. He woke up, screaming. He'd seen other visions, he told Mary the next morning. He'd met a figure, who was himself, walking on the terrace, who said to him, "How long do you mean to be content?"

On May 12 Shelley's new boat had arrived from Genoa. Byron appointed himself to name it—the *Don Juan*. In June they heard that the Hunts, about whom Mary had been so worried, had finally arrived in Italy and were heading for Livorno. On July 1, Shelley and Williams set sail for Livorno to meet them.

When Shelley arrived he wrote Mary a letter:

> How are you, my best Mary? Write especially how is your health and how your spirits are, and whether you are not more reconciled to staying at Lerici, at least during the summer.
>
> You have no idea how I am hurried and occupied; I have not a moment's leisure but will write by next post. Ever, dearest Mary, Yours affectionately—S.
>
> I have found the translation of the "Symposium."

It was the last letter she ever received from him.

All week, Mary had been almost sick with irrational worry for young Percy's health. Three of her children had died. Why should this one be any different? She was an emotional wreck, still not recovered, physically or emotionally, from her miscarriage. Shelley's absence increased her fears. She cried bitterly when he left. If he were home and anything happened to the baby, he would somehow save him, keep him alive. She paced the terrace, staring

145

out at the beautiful bay, the castles that encircled it, the moon, and the wild waves, and longed for Shelley's return.

On Saturday, Jane received a note from Edward. They would leave Livorno on Monday; expect them by Tuesday night. Monday turned out to be wild and stormy, so Mary and Jane assumed they'd wait to start out. Tuesday continued rainy, but Wednesday and Thursday were calm and fair. Anxiously the two women looked for the boat's tall sail to round the promontory. When Thursday evening came and their husbands still didn't return, the women feared one of the men had fallen ill and was too sick to travel. Jane was so anxious she decided to have someone row her to Livorno on Friday. But the waves swelled so high, no boats would venture out.

A letter from Leigh Hunt arrived addressed to Shelley. Mary tore it open: "Pray write to tell us how you got home, for they say that you had bad weather after you sailed Monday and we are anxious." The letter dropped from her hands. She trembled all over. Jane picked it up and read it.

"Then it's all over," she said.

"No, my dear Jane," Mary cried, "it is not all over, but this suspense is dreadful. Come with me. We will go to Leghorn . . . and learn our fate."

They went by land, changing horses at each stop, as Mary had traveled when she and Shelley eloped to France eager to escape pursuit. Now she and Jane were speeding over the roads, heedless of the tossing and shaking of the coach, stopping first at Lerici, where they learned that no accident had been reported, then straight on south to Pisa.

It was midnight when they reached Byron's villa. Mary jumped out of the coach as the driver pounded on the door. A maid answered. Wild and disheveled, Mary staggered up the stairs, so deadly white that Byron and his mistress thought they were looking at a ghost. She could hardly speak. "Where is he?" she managed to ask.

They knew nothing, only that Shelley had left Pisa on Sunday and sailed from Livorno on Monday, and that on Monday afternoon a storm had broken out. Mary and Jane refused to rest. They scrambled back into the coach and headed toward the coast. It was two in the morning when they reached the inn at Livorno, where either Trelawny or his friend Roberts was supposed to be. It was the wrong inn. They would have to wait until morning.

The women flung themselves across the beds and slept fitfully until six, then went from inn to inn until they found Roberts at the Globe. He came down to greet them, his face troubled.

Shelley and Edward, he said, had spent Monday morning buying provisions. A morning thunderstorm passed and the weather cleared with a good wind for home. Roberts had suggested they wait another day to be sure the weather had settled, but they were impatient to be on their way. At one o'clock they had sailed. Shelley had been in one of his exuberant fits of good spirits. Roberts watched them from the dock.

Two hours later a storm blew up. Roberts climbed a tower and searched for them with his telescope. He spotted them about ten miles out to sea, taking in their topsails. Then the storm obscured them. When it cleared, instead of seeing them return as he expected, they were gone.

Mary refused to give up hope. Perhaps they had been driven to an offshore island and lost their bearings. She and Jane would head home after making sure the towers along the coast were alerted to look for the missing men.

On the way home they found that a small boat and a water cask from the *Don Juan* had been discovered. Mary tried to reassure herself that perhaps they'd thrown them overboard in the stormy weather. They waited at home through five days of hope and fear. Trelawny stayed with them. On July 18, he returned to Livorno, seeking news. At seven the next night he returned. The bodies had been found, washed up on shore.

Italian quarantine laws would not allow the bodies to be taken away to be buried. They had to be cremated on the beach. So on August 15, 1822, Byron, Trelawny, and Leigh Hunt constructed a funeral pyre on the beach near Viareggio and burned Edward Williams' corpse. The next day they did the same for Shelley.

It was a grisly business. Shelley's heart wouldn't burn. Trelawny snatched it from the fire and gave it to Hunt, who, eventually, at Mary's insistence, gave it to her. Shelley's ashes were buried in the Protestant Cemetery at Rome where William had been buried, although the little boy's grave could not be found.

Remembering Shelley's delight when he had quoted the lines from Shakespeare, Trelawny chose them for the inscription on his memorial stone:

> Nothing of him that doth fade,
> But doth suffer a sea-change,
> Into something rich and strange.

FIFTEEN

Going Home

This morn thy gallant bark, Love,
   Sailed on a sunny sea;
'Tis noon, and tempests dark, Love,
   Have wrecked it on the lee.
. . . . . .
O list! O list! O list!
   The Spirits of the deep—
Loud sounds their wail of sorrow—
   While I for ever weep!

      —from "The Dirge" by Mary Shelley

Mary spent a year in Italy with her friends the Hunts, grieving for Shelley and feeling guilty. She blamed herself for the depressed spirits she hadn't been able to shake after the death of her children. She blamed herself for being cold to Shelley and withdrawing into herself, for allowing their relationship to decline from that perfect sympathy they'd enjoyed in earlier years. She wrote poems like "The Dirge" to ease her troubled spirit. For the rest of her life, Shelley's death would be inspiration and subject matter for her work.

She dreamed of him. Once she thought she heard him call her name. Another day, as she was looking out over the water, she saw a white sail in the distance and for a moment thought, *There they are! I will take a boat and go out to them.* But it was all cruel illusion. Mary poured her grief into her journal. "He is gone—the sun of my existence, the animating spark of my life. The companion, friend, lover, husband. And I am deserted. A frightful vista of long drawn out years is before me."

She took stock. She was twenty-five years old, the widowed mother of a three-year-old son. What was she to do with the rest of her life? She had three goals. First, to give her son a good education and bring him up to be a credit to his father. Second, to go on living in Italy—or even France or Switzerland. Anywhere but cold, damp, prudish, and unforgiving England. Third, to publish her husband's life and works. Shelley, spurned as an immoral radical, was little known in England. A new edition of his poetry and a biography would go a long way toward giving him the fame she knew he deserved. She might have achieved her goals easily if it weren't for the enmity of her father-in-law, Sir Timothy Shelley, who did all he could to thwart her. She was in for a long, hard struggle.

Shelley had left her no money—only a share in the family estate, which she couldn't collect until Sir Timothy was dead. She planned to live by writing, a precarious way of life. With a child to care for, she needed a steady means of support. Byron, as one of the executor's of Shelley's estate, asked Sir Timothy for a yearly allowance for his grandson and daughter-in-law.

But Sir Timothy was deeply angered. He had never forgiven his son for hurting him so badly—spurning his values, making him look like a fool. His clever boy with his "literary turn" had flaunted radicalism, married beneath him, left his wife to run off with someone else, disgraced the family name. Sir Timothy wished that he could forget his only son had ever lived. And he wanted everyone else to forget him too. Like many parents, he blamed others for his child's behavior. It was Mary, he was sure, with her radical Godwinian upbringing, who had lured Shelley away from his marriage. (Just as William Godwin had always blamed Shelley for seducing Mary.) Sir Timothy believed that Mary had "estranged my son's mind from his family, and all his first duties in life."

Although Sir Timothy refused to give Mary money, he did make her an offer. He would not have his grandson under his own roof, but he would support him if Mary were willing to put him into the care of English guardians. Otherwise, no.

Byron, not known for his parental feelings, thought Mary should accept. But she would not give up her son. As she wrote to her and Shelley's old friend Thomas Jefferson Hogg, "he is my all. My other children I have lost, and the pangs I endured when those events happened were so terrible, that even now, inured as I am to mental pain, I look back with affright to those periods of agony. . . . I could not live a day without my boy."

So she decided to return to chilly England, where earning money would be easier. Perhaps also, if she could see Sir Timothy personally, he would change his mind. Yet leaving Italy was hard. She confided in Shelley through her journal. "I would never leave this sky—this earth—

151

even this sea, which forces me, for your sake, to love it, but that I must on our child's account."

On July 25, 1823, Mary and Percy left Genoa for the long journey home over land and sea. One month later, they stepped off the London wharf into the welcoming arms of her father and half-brother William, who had grown into a young man of twenty and trained as an engineer, though he would soon make writing his career. Aside from Mrs. G., they were the only members of her family still in England. Claire was in Vienna with Charles Clairmont, her brother and Mary's stepbrother, who was a teacher there.

To Mary, England seemed like a foreign country. "The names of the places sound strangely, the voices of the people are new and grating," she wrote to Leigh Hunt in Italy, "but for my father, I should be with you next spring." Now that Godwin had his daughter back, he didn't want to let her go.

Godwin encouraged Mary to support herself by writing. "Your talents are truly extraordinary. *Frankenstein* is universally known, and . . . is the most wonderful book to have been written at twenty years of age that I ever heard of . . . fortunately you have pursued a course of reading, and cultivated your mind in the manner most admirably adapted to make you a great and successful author. If you cannot be independent, who should be?"

It's true that upon returning to England, "Lo and behold! I found myself famous!" A playwright, Richard Brinsley Peake, had written a popular play, *Presumption, or the Fate of Frankenstein,* based on her novel, which was playing at the English opera house. On August 29, she saw it with her father, brother, and Jane Williams. A novelist today would have cause for legal action and probably be outraged to find that someone had made a play of her work without asking permission or offering compensation. But Mary was delighted and thought it well acted. The monster, to whom she had given no name, was listed in the playbill as "_____." "This nameless mode of naming the unnameable is rather good," she said. The actor who played him had a blue body, greenish face, black lips, and wore a toga. Mary wrote:

> [Frankenstein] is at the beginning full of hope and expectation. At the end of the 1st Act the stage represents a room with a staircase leading to F[rankenstein]'s workshop. He goes to it and you see his light at a small window, through which a frightened servant peeps, who runs off in terror when F exclaims "It lives!" Presently F himself rushes in horror and trepidation from the room and while still expressing his agony and terror _____ [the monster] throws down the door of the laboratory, leaps the staircase and presents his unearthly and monstrous person on the stage. [The actor] played _____'s part extremely well—his seeking as it were for support, his trying to grasp at the sounds he heard, all indeed he does was well imagined and executed. I was much amused, and it appeared to excite a breathless eagerness in the audience.

It's interesting that she focused on this scene, the first one she had thought of when the idea for the story came to her. Even though presented differently on stage from the way she'd imagined and written it, the moment of the monster's birth must have remained for her the most significant. The addition of a servant for Frankenstein was new, and would later appear in films.

Mary wrote Sir Timothy at once to see what he would do for his grandson. The answer was, not much. He wouldn't even meet with her, but negotiated through his lawyer. He loaned her a hundred pounds for expenses and promised as much a year toward Percy's support. It was enough to keep them from starving, but little more. And when she finally did come into her inheritance, she would have to pay the allowance back to the estate.

Sir Timothy's direct heir was Charles, Shelley's son by Harriet. Orphaned now, Charles and his sister, Ianthe, lived with their paternal grandparents at Field Place, the Shelley family estate. Three years after Mary's return, when Percy was not quite seven, Charles died of tuberculosis, and Percy became his grandfather's heir, a future baronet and master of Field Place.

Even this didn't do much to soften the old man. After a year of haggling, he agreed to advance Mary 250 pounds a year, to be increased as needed to pay for Percy's education. Sir Timothy and Lady Shelley arranged to visit their grandson. It pained Sir Timothy to see how much the boy looked like his father. Yet the old man liked Percy and saw him from time to time after that.

In 1823 Mary collected and edited sixty-five of her husband's previously unpublished poems and published them in a volume called *Posthumous Poems of Percy Bysshe Shelley.* In the preface, she defended Shelley's radicalism. He had been "pursued by hatred and calumny," she said, because of "his fearless enthusiasm" for improving "the moral and physical state of mankind." During the short time that it was available, the book did what she wanted it to. People read and admired Shelley's work. Although many still condemned him, others called him an immortal genius.

When Sir Timothy found out, he forced her to recall all the unsold copies and to give up plans for writing Shelley's life. She'd hoped a biography would clear his name completely and make people realize he hadn't been an ordinary adulterous husband when he left Harriet for her, but rather someone acting on principle. Now she would have to put off her plans while Sir Timothy lived. "No great harm," she told herself, "since he is above 70." Whenever she heard that Sir Timothy was sick, she would begin to gather her materials. But somehow the old man always got well.

In the meantime, she earned her living writing novels, short stories, and nonfiction. *Valperga,* a historical novel begun in 1820 in Pisa, was published in 1823. The next year she began *The Last Man.* Set in the future, it tells of an epidemic that eventually wipes out everyone in the world. The main character, Verney, is based on Mary; Adrian, on Shelley; and Raymond, on Byron.

The title page of *The Last Man* didn't give her name, just "by the author of *Frankenstein.*" Even though the first edition of *Frankenstein* had been published anonymously, reviews of *The Last Man* referred to Mary Shelley as its author. Sir Timothy was so angry to see the Shelley name in print that he suspended her allowance, even though it wasn't her fault.

In *The Fortunes of Perkin Warbeck,* a historical novel written in 1829, she based the character of Lady Katherine Gordon on herself. *Lodore,* published in 1835 and also biographical, recalls the desperate time when Shelley was running from debtor's prison. In 1837 she published *Falkner,* the last of her novels. None equal *Frankenstein* in power and originality. *The Last Man,* also a science fiction novel, comes closest. She brought out a revised edition of *Frankenstein* in 1831.

Despite her fame, her work, and her closeness to her father and son, Mary was lonely. In June 1824 she moved to Kentish Town to be near Jane Williams, who'd also returned to England. Ever since their husbands' deaths, the two had drawn close. Jane became Mary's "sole delight." "I have been serene, often happy," Mary wrote in her journal after they spent a month together in Brighton. "Happy when with Jane, happy while studying Greek. If I were sixty I have no great cause to repine. I need only forget that I am not half that age—not an easy thing. Nevertheless for the greater part of this time I have been at peace."

A year later, Mary discovered that Jane had been spreading stories about her for years, from even before they'd left Italy, saying that Mary had been a bad wife to Shelley, stressing how close *she* and Shelley had been. As a result, Mary's friends tended to lack sympathy for her grief, believing her loss not real. Hogg, who was to become Jane's lover and husband, was convinced that Mary and Shelley had been on the verge of breaking up.

Mary was devastated. "My friend has proved false and treacherous!" she told her journal. "Miserable discovery. For four years I was devoted to her and I earned only ingratitude. . . . Am I not a fool! What deadly cold flows through my veins." It was months before she could bring herself to tell Jane that she knew. When she tried, Jane broke into tears before she could finish, so Mary wrote her feelings in a letter. Although they remained friends of a sort, Mary could never fully forgive her.

Still an attractive young woman, Mary might have remarried. A friend described her "well-shaped, golden-haired head, almost always a little bent and drooping . . . marble-white shoulders and arms . . . thoughtful, earnest eyes" and "white, dimpled, small hands, with rosy palms, and plumply commencing fingers, that tapered into tips as slender and delicate as those in a Vandyke portrait." Another said she was "cool, quiet and feminine to the last degree—I mean in delicacy of manner and expression."

Sometimes she despaired, "I never shall be loved more—never o never more shall I love . . . never more shall I be happy—never more feel life sit triumphant in my frame." But men did fall in love with her and propose marriage, including John Howard Payne, the American song-writer and author of "Home, Sweet Home." She briefly became infatuated with American writer Washington Irving, but nothing came of it.

Mary spent the fourteen years following Shelley's death raising her son, writing her books, editing Shelley's work, trying to maintain her friendships, and fighting with her father-in-law, who made almost everything else she attempted difficult or impossible. They had been years of struggle, but she met them with intelligence, honesty, and courage. As she entered her forties, she came at last into a late flowering, fulfilling, at least in part, some of the desires of her heart, not only to raise her son, but to earn money by writing, to memorialize Shelley, to return to Italy.

SIXTEEN

A Late Flowering

This may often be observed with women. . . . As years are added they gather courage; they feel the earth grow steadier under their steps; they depend less on others. . . .

—from *Lives of the Most Eminent Literary and Scientific Men of France* by Mary Shelley

During the early spring of 1836, when Mary was thirty-eight, she was summoned to her father's bedside. Eighty-year-old William Godwin was dying. Mary and Mrs. G., having made peace at last, took turns caring for him. Both were with him when his heart stopped.

All he had to leave his seventy-year-old wife was 100 pounds and the news that, despite their contented thirty-five-year marriage, he wished to be buried next to Mary Wollstonecraft, still his one true love after all these years.

He had named Mary the executor of his estate, leaving her a mass of papers to sift through and instructions to publish his last book, an anti-Christian work called *The*

Genius of Christianity Unveiled. But Mary's first loyalty was to her son, who was about to enter Cambridge University. Publishing a radical book now would cause a public outcry and hurt his chances to make friends and have a normal life. "I must see him fairly launched," Mary wrote, "before I commit myself to the fury of the waves."

Her son Percy, blessed with his father's staring blue eyes, was the main focus of Mary's emotions. When he was eleven, she wrote that he was "growing more and more like Shelley." A man who knew the family said of Percy, "If talent descended, what ought he not be, he who is the blood of Godwin, Mrs. Wollstonecraft, Shelley and Mrs. Shelley!" But in Percy's case, talent hadn't descended. Despite his looks, which coarsened as he grew older, and Mary's great love for him, she couldn't help but feel that Percy was a bit of a disappointment. To Maria Gisborne, she admitted that he wasn't much like his father or her. He lacked "sensibility." All he shared with his father, to her terror, was a love of boats.

Percy was a stolid youth who remained undistinguished all his life. Unlike Mary, he didn't let the fact of his famous parentage pressure him into any attempt at imitating them. Perhaps he knew it would be no use. Perhaps it was just easier not to try.

Determined to see that Percy got a good education, despite the cost, Mary had sent him to Harrow, which, like Eton, where Shelley had suffered so much, was one of England's great public schools. He studied mainly grammar, composition, Latin, and Greek—a traditional education. Friends accused Mary of becoming conventional. Didn't she want Percy to learn to think for himself? someone supposedly asked her. And Mary is supposed to have replied, "Oh God, teach him to think like other people."

Although this story may not be true, Mary did change as she grew older and more experienced. She shed some of the values she had picked up from her parents, her friends, and Shelley, and discovered what she herself really believed.

In 1838, when she was accused of not carrying on the radical work of her parents and Shelley, she answered the criticism in her journal. "With regard to the 'good cause'—the cause of the advancement of freedom and knowledge—of the rights of women, etc., I am not a person of opinions. . . . If I have never written to vindicate the rights of women, I have ever befriended women when oppressed." Which was perfectly true.

She followed her father's philosophy that money must be shared with those who need it. But unlike Godwin, she emphasized giving to others, not getting herself. Even when she had little money, she always gave if she possibly could, often denying herself to help the Godwins and Claire, Jane Williams, and many others, even Aunt Everina Wollstonecraft, whom no one much liked.

Despite her great respect for them, she was not her mother, not her father, not her late husband. "I am instable, sometimes melancholy and have been called on occasions imperious. But I never did an ungracious act in my life. I sympathize warmly with others. I have wasted my heart in their love and service."

After *Falkner*, Mary wrote no more novels. Instead, she became a respected writer of biographies for a series called the *Cabinet Cyclopaedia*, beginning with the lives of

Italian authors Francesco Petrarch, Giovanni Boccaccio, and Niccolò Machiavelli for the first volume of the *Lives of the Most Eminent Literary Men of Italy, Spain and Portugal*. She mentions this work in her letters more than she does any of her other writing. She would probably have been a scholar in the professional sense if she'd lived in later times.

In 1838 she again decided to prepare an edition of Shelley's collected poetry and to write his biography. She asked Sir Timothy, still alive at eighty-five, for permission. He said yes to the poems, but no to the biography. She thought up a scheme to outflank him, at least in part, by adding notes to the poems describing the inner and outer circumstances of Shelley's life when he wrote each one. Readers, scholars, and critics have been grateful for *The Poetical Works of Percy Bysshe Shelley* ever since. Through this work, she achieved her goal of establishing Shelley as one of England's greatest poets.

At this time, she became close to Aubrey Beauclerk, a man near her age, a recent widower with four children. They talked of marrying once his mourning for his wife eased. The relationship perked her up. In November 1839 she wrote in her journal: "A friendship secure, helpful—enduring—a union with a generous heart—and yet a suffering one whom I may comfort and bless. . . . I can indeed confide in A's unalterable gentleness and true affection but will not events place us asunder?. . . We shall see!"

In the meantime, she traveled. In 1840, Percy, "the dearest treasure ever Mother was blest with," was in his last year at Cambridge. During his summer holiday, Mary traveled with him and two college friends to Paris, then

MARY SHELLEY

through Germany to Lake Como in Italy, the first time she'd been back in seventeen years. "I feel a good deal of the gypsy coming upon me," she said. For eight weeks they stayed at an inn. While the young men studied, Mary read, embroidered, and wrote letters. She hated the thought of returning to England except that Aubrey was there.

Percy and his friends returned to England and Cambridge in September, but Mary stayed on a little longer, traveling about. She went to Paris, where she saw Claire and other old friends. Perhaps they talked of Byron, who had died almost twenty years before. She then went to Switzerland to visit the shores of Lake Leman, where she had once been so happy, where Byron had read his ghost stories, and where the idea for *Frankenstein* had been conceived.

At length, I caught a glimpse of the scenes among which I had lived, when first I stepped out from childhood into life. There, on the shores of Bellerive, stood Diodati; and our humble dwelling, Maison Chapuis, nestled close to the lake below. There were the terraces, the vineyards, the upward path threading them, the little port where our boat lay moored; I could mark and recognize a thousand slight peculiarities, familiar objects then—forgotten since—now replete with recollections and associations.

[A]ll my life since was but an unreal phantasmagoria—the shades that gathered round that scene were the realities. . . .

In Paris she discovered that her last chance at married happiness had fled. Back in England Aubrey Beauclerk

163

had married Rosa Robinson, a poor young woman whom Mary had once supported. Mary returned to London "un-happy—betrayed, alone!"

For three years, she traveled back and forth to the Continent—to Italy, Germany, and France. She would have liked to live in Italy, but to Percy only England was home. He was all she had left. Where he lived, she would live too. In 1844 she published *Rambles in Germany and Italy*, her last major work.

In that same year her old enemy, Sir Timothy, "Old Sir Tim or rather Eternity," finally died at age ninety; Percy, now Sir Percy, inherited his considerable estate. He and Mary decided to share its income equally. For once in her life, she could depend upon a decent sum of money, enough to give a great deal away to those who needed it more.

Deep in her heart, Mary had always hoped her son would reflect the glory of his parentage. But, perhaps re-membering the effect such pressure had had on her, when she saw that he was not the reincarnation of his fa-ther, she learned to accept him for the qualities he had. Percy was neither particularly intelligent nor creative, just a short, stout, sweet, and simple man who "put on an air of stupidity" when his mother tried to introduce him to distinguished people. On their second trip to Italy, his mother had complained that he avoided girls and society in general, was rather lazy, and showed no interest in his-tory or art. He lacked his mother's ease and social charm, but he loved her deeply.

In 1848 Percy married Jane St. John, a twenty-eight-year-old widow, short and plump, affectionate, energetic, and brave. The new Lady Shelley adored her new mother-in-law, and Mary took to her at once. "A prize indeed," she said, "the best and sweetest thing in the world."

The young couple invited Mary to live with them at Field Place, where Shelley had grown up. She chose his bedroom for herself. Here she could look out on the same lawns and trees he had looked upon as a boy. She could indulge in dreams and exercise her imagination, as she had loved to do since she was a girl.

Once while reading through her journal, Mary noticed how full it seemed of her unhappiness and complaints. She was struck by "what a very imperfect picture . . . these querulous pages afford of me. This arises from their being the record of my feelings, and not of my imagination." Imagination, the ability to dream, was her "stately pleasure ground," the one constant source of happiness in her life.

SEVENTEEN

The Graveyard

I go to no new creation, I enter under no new laws.
The God that made this beautiful world made that
into which I go; as there is beauty & love here,
such is there and I felt as if my spirit would when it
left my frame be received and sustained by a bene-
ficient and gentle power. I had no fear. . . .

—from an October 5, 1839, entry in Mary
Shelley's journal

In 1848 Mary developed strange symptoms—dizziness
and "swimming" in her head, difficulty in concentrat-
ing, pain in her legs, head, and one eye. The headaches
grew worse. Sometimes her arm seemed paralyzed. Other
times her arm and leg shook.

No one knew what was wrong. One doctor recommended cod-liver oil and visits to the seashore. Another
had her sip wine. In fact, a tumor, not diagnosed until
1850, was growing in her brain. Her daughter-in-law Jane
was ill too. Field Place was damp. Percy bought a new

house, Boscombe Manor, in Bournemouth, a resort on England's southern coast.

When Mary learned that she was dying, she and Jane decided to keep the truth from Percy for as long as they could. Mary was not afraid to die; she had lost her fear of death years ago when she had come so close to dying from her miscarriage. "Whether the nature of my illness—debility from loss of blood, without pain—caused this tranquillity of soul, I cannot tell; but so it was, and it had this blessed effect, that I have never since anticipated death with terror. . . ."

When her old friend Edward Trelawny heard of Mary's impending death, he offered to give her the grave next to Shelley's, which he owned. She said no. Transporting her body to Rome would take too much trouble and money.

Mary died on February 1, 1851, at the age of fifty-three, in Chester Square, the Shelleys' London home. She had asked to be buried next to her mother and father in St. Pancras churchyard, where she had so often spent her afternoons as a girl, and where she and Shelley had declared their love for each other. But the once pleasantly green and leafy churchyard was now hemmed in by one of London's ugliest neighborhoods. Lady Shelley said, "it would have broken my heart to let her loveliness wither in such a dreadful place."

Mary would lie next to her parents, but in Bournemouth, not London. Jane had the bodies of William Godwin and Mary Wollstonecraft exhumed and transported to Bournemouth to be reburied with their daughter in nearby St. Peter's churchyard. The body of Mrs. G., the second Mrs. Godwin, who had also died and been buried next to the famous pair, she left behind.

The rector of St. Peter's, however, said he wouldn't bury the corpses of three such scandalous people, heretics and unbelievers all. Lady Shelley had the three coffins placed in the hearse anyway. Sending it on ahead, she and Percy climbed into a carriage and followed behind. When both carriages reached the churchyard's locked iron gates, they stopped. They would stay there, she informed the rector, until the bodies were allowed in.

The rector had no choice. The gravedigger went to work. By nighttime, with no ceremony, the bodies were lowered into a grave.

When the time came to inscribe the tomb, the rector objected to the words "Author of 'Vindication of the Rights of Woman'" which Lady Shelley wanted under Wollstonecraft's name. It was a wicked book, he said. Jane asked if he'd ever read it. He hadn't. Well then, he'd better read it before objecting. She sent him a copy, he read it, agreed he could find no fault with it, and allowed the words to be inscribed.

Under Godwin's name, Jane had inscribed, "Author of *Political Justice.*" Under Mary's, however, she inscribed only the names of her famous parents and "Widow of the late Percy Bysshe Shelley." Her authorship of *Frankenstein* went unrecorded.

On the first anniversary of Mary's death, Percy and Jane opened the box-desk Mary had kept at her bedside. They found her most cherished treasures—locks of her dead children's hair, a workbook she and Shelley had shared, and Shelley's copy of his long poem *Adonais,* a lament for the early death of the poet John Keats.

A page torn from the poem had been wrapped around a piece of silk. Carefully unwrapping it, they found some of Shelley's ashes and the remains of his heart, snatched from the funeral pyre as the rest of his body burned to ashes. Doctors now believe that Shelley suffered from a disease that turned his heart muscle into calcium, causing intense pain. That was why remains still existed of his "heart of stone."

Lady Shelley kept the heart in a small silver urn. When Percy died thirty-eight years later and was buried in the tomb with his mother and grandparents, she took advantage of the grave being open to place Shelley's heart next to the body of his wife.

Most of the London young Mary Godwin knew has vanished. Skinner Street lies buried under the Holborn Viaduct. Rows of small brick council houses cover the fields of what was once Somers Town. But old St. Pancras Church and its tombstone-covered churchyard still exist, looking very much as they did 200 years ago when Mary haunted them.

The church is still in use: *Parish Church of Saint Pancras (Old Church),* the sign says. *Church of England Masses Sun. Tues. Th. Sat.* It is the most ancient building in the borough. According to a plaque on the church gate, parts of it belong to the eleventh century and contain Roman tiles. Its altar stone dates from the early seventh century and was probably used by St. Augustine. Across the side of the church someone has spray painted the word *STARK.*

The former graveyard, backed up against the railroad tracks and fronted by a heavily trafficked road, is now a South Camden neighborhood park. A modern public health center and a coroner's court are set off in a back corner. On a November day, the dirt paths are covered by a blanket of wet autumn leaves from the towering oaks that form a canopy overhead. Squirrels scamper about. Besides the few scattered wooden benches, some rubber tires hang by ropes from the branches of trees. A class of kindergartners and their teachers walk through the park. Young mothers with baby strollers sit on a bench and soak up what they can of the pale November sun.

In the mid-nineteenth century when the Metropolitan and Midland Railways were built, the graves were moved and gardens were formed. The old tombstones are scattered about under the huge oaks and a blanket of brown and yellow leaves. Moss covers their stone tops. Many are toppled over. Most have been so worn away by time that the inscriptions—many dating from the late 1700s—have been erased. A monument lists the obliterated names.

Though the bodies of Mary's parents have been moved, their tombstone remains, capped with moss, stained gray from damp, inscribed on three sides:

Mary Wollstonecraft Godwin
Author of A Vindication of the Rights of Woman
Born 27th April 1759
Died 10th September 1797

William Godwin
Author of Political Justice
Born 3rd March 1756
Died 7th April 1836
Aged 80 years

Mary Jane
Second Wife of
William Godwin
Died 17th June 1841
Aged 75 years

Behind its ornate wrought-iron gates, the old church of St. Pancras and its oak-shaded burial ground seem like a haven of quiet in a bustling city. Two hundred years ago, it probably seemed that way to young Mary Godwin too. It is easy to imagine that pale, slender girl still haunting her mother's empty grave, still weaving stories in the air to drive away loneliness, still reveling in her "darling sun bright dreams."

EPILOGUE

My Hideous Progeny

Like one, that on a lonesome road
Doth walk in fear and dread,
And having once turned round walks on,
And turns no more his head;
Because he knows, a frightful fiend
Doth close behind him tread.

—from "The Rime of the Ancient Mariner" by
Samuel Taylor Coleridge

L ady Shelley carried on the work of memorialization.
She collected information about her famous in-laws,
interviewed people who had known them, and published
the *Shelley Memorials*. Mary Shelley's room became a kind
of shrine. Sir Percy's unremarkable life with its boats and
plays continued to its natural end. He and Lady Shelley
had no children. The line of Godwin and Wollstonecraft,
Shelley and Mary, died out with him.

Though Mary Shelley left no physical descendents, her
fictional offspring, the "hideous progeny" she spawned,

have flourished ever since. In plays, movies, and on television, Dr. Victor Frankenstein and his monster live on. In retelling her story, however, part of its essential theme has been distorted. The *Frankenstein* that Mary Shelley created is not the *Frankenstein* most of us know.

Starting with *Presumption,* which Mary saw and described in 1823, countless plays based on her novel have been produced. The nineteenth-century actor Walter Cooke became famous for his portrayal of the juicy role of the monster.

Plays kept *Frankenstein* alive in the popular imagination. But it wasn't until the movies revisioned the story that it became one of our most powerful myths. More than forty film versions were produced between 1910 and 1994, starting with a silent film Charles Ogle made for Edison studios. It was James Whale's 1931 version starring Boris Karloff as the monster, however, that created the *Frankenstein* most people know. The role made Karloff famous and etched his version of the monster on the public psyche.

Whale's version, in which the actors wear clothes of the 1920s and 30s, although they rely on torches for light, is based more on the earlier plays than on the novel. As in the version Mary saw, Frankenstein has an assistant, a comic figure. Sent to steal a human brain from a medical lab, he grabs an abnormal one by mistake. Instead of creating his monster from various body parts, Frankenstein simply inserts the pilfered brain into the corpse of a recently hanged criminal.

The actual animation of the monster, the details of which are left vague in the novel, is the movie's big scene.

As a storm rages outside, Frankenstein invites his fiancée, his best friend, and a professor from the university into his cavernous stone-walled laboratory. Amidst the roar of thunder and crackle of lightning, a platform raises the creature up to the skylight, where, struck by bolts of lightning, it quivers to life. No one is horrified by the monster's ugliness. Frankenstein is proud of his success, complacent even, and defends what he has done.

Although the movie's plot is based on earlier dramatizations, the character of the monster springs straight from the pages of Mary's book. Karloff's acting and makeup capture the monster's yearning, vulnerability, spirit, and pathos. But by the end of the film, when he attacks Frankenstein's bride for no apparent reason, the monster has become totally evil.

The townspeople hunt him through the nighttime countryside with dogs and torches, like the kind of lynch mob familiar to early twentieth-century viewers. No blame attaches to Victor, who is seen as misguided but well-meaning; he strove to create, but his creation turned against him. The mob sets ablaze the wooden windmill where the monster is hiding, signaling the victory of virtuous humanity over the evil nonhuman.

The movie was such a success that Whale produced a sequel in 1935, *The Bride of Frankenstein,* which many people consider a classic. In it, Elsa Lancaster plays both a female monster and, in the opening scene, Mary Shelley herself, at the Villa Diodati with Shelley and Byron, explaining that the monster hadn't really died at all.

Since then, cheerfully mixing up monster and maker, the story has descended into caricature and comedy, popping up in TV's *The Munsters* and in cartoons, games, toys, and commercials as well as film. There have been a son, daughter, house, and ghost of Frankenstein, and a lady, a young, and a teenage Frankenstein too. Frankenstein has met the Wolfman, the Space Monster, and Abbott and Costello. In 1966 Jesse James met Frankenstein's daughter. Frankenstein has created woman and conquered the world.

A 1982 version made for British television has touches of authenticity—there's no lifting the body to the skylight, for example—but its theme still reflects the plays more than the book. Frankenstein isn't horrified by his creation and doesn't flee from it. Instead, the monster flees from him. At the very end, after he has killed Victor's bride, the monster says, "You gave me life. Why didn't you give me a soul?"

"Because I am not God," Frankenstein replies.

Except for its grotesque ending, Kenneth Branagh's 1994 movie, *Mary Shelley's Frankenstein,* with Robert DeNiro as the monster, sticks close to the original, with some changes for dramatic effect. It opens in the Arctic, with Walton rescuing Frankenstein from the maddened pursuit of his creature. And the comic assistant is gone. But this version also lets Frankenstein off the hook. Although after bringing the monster to life he is suddenly appalled at what he has done, he can't be blamed for abandoning the monster because he thinks the monster is dead.

In Mary Shelley's original version, Justine, the servant accused of killing young William, is brought to trial. Although Victor knows that she is innocent, he doesn't try to save her. No one would believe his story of an eight-foot monster, he decides, and besides, he'd end up looking like a fool. So he does nothing, and Justine is condemned and hanged. In Branagh's movie, however, he is truly unable to save her because she is lynched by a mob before she comes to trial.

In the movie, although at first Victor agrees to make a bride for the monster, he changes his mind when the monster brings him Justine's body to use—again excusing him and putting the blame on the monster. When the monster kills Elizabeth, Frankenstein puts her brain into Justine's body (and botches the job badly, for she ends up with hideous stitching across her face for some reason), but she refuses to live like this and kills herself.

Yet whatever shape it takes, Mary Shelley's tale has an enduring popularity. Frankenstein and his monster have achieved the status of archetype, or myth. They contain such a significant truth about human nature that we cannot refrain from enacting it in one form or another over and over again. Even movies like *Jurassic Park* and *Honey, I Shrunk the Kids* are variations on what has come to be seen as the essential Frankenstein myth—a scientist who overreaches himself to create something harmful and out of control.

What is unusual about the Frankenstein myth is its youth. Most of the archetypes we reenact—the hero's quest, the rebirth of the dead god—come from ancient sources, such as the Bible and Greek mythology. Although there have been some Frankenstein-like stories in the past—such as the Jewish myth of the golem—the true archetype arose with the birth of modern science.

Frankenstein's monster is not horrible just because he is a dead man brought back to life—that we find fearful enough, as the archetypes of vampires and zombies show—but because he is a thing, created by science, not magic, out of dead body parts, soulless but alive.

Frankenstein was born out of the fear of humanity's new power. We fear the monster because we fear the scientist's ability to control the mysteries at the heart of nature—birth, life, and death. To fiddle with the mechanisms that produce life seems both blasphemous and unnatural. Yet scientists do it all the time, and we accept the benefits. We want the power, but fear it too.

The form of the myth shown in plays and movies focuses on Victor Frankenstein's folly in going against nature. His mistake lies in creating the monster. From then on he is portrayed as a doomed, tragic hero, helpless before the forces he has created.

But Mary Shelley's novel is more subtle. Frankenstein is at fault not for creating the monster, but for neglecting to take responsibility for it. As we wrestle with issues of cloning, genetic engineering, prolonging life, test-tube babies, and the like, perhaps her version of the myth is the one we should remember.

Chronology of Mary Shelley's Life

1797	Mary Godwin born in London. Mary Wollstonecraft dies.
1801	William Godwin marries Mary Jane Clairmont.
1808	Mary's poem "Mounseer Nongtongpaw" published.
1812–1813	Mary lives in Scotland with the Baxters.
1814	Mary and Percy Bysshe Shelley elope to France.
1815	Mary's premature baby girl dies.
1816	Mary's son William is born.
	At the Villa Diodati, Mary conceives the idea for *Frankenstein*.
	Fanny Godwin and Harriet Shelley commit suicide.
	Mary and Shelley marry in England.
1817	Claire Clairmont gives birth to Byron's daughter, Alba.
	Shelley loses custody of his children.

1817	Mary finishes *Frankenstein* and gives birth to Clara Everina.
1818	*Frankenstein* is published.
	One-year-old Clara Everina dies in Italy.
1819	Three-year-old William dies.
	Mary gives birth to Percy Florence.
1822	Claire and Byron's daughter Allegra dies.
	Shelley drowns off the coast of Italy.
1823	Mary returns to England with her son Percy.
	Sir Timothy Shelley stops the publication of Mary's edition of Shelley's unpublished poems.
1831	Mary publishes a revised edition of *Frankenstein.*
1836	William Godwin dies.
1839	Mary publishes Shelley's *Poetical Works,* with biographical notes.
1840–1843	Mary travels in Europe.
1844	Sir Timothy dies and Percy inherits the estate.
1849	Mary moves into Field Place with Percy and his new wife, Jane.
1851	Mary dies at age fifty-three and is buried in Bournemouth next to the exhumed bodies of her parents.

Selected Bibliography

Barzun, Jacques. *Classic, Romantic and Modern.* Chicago: University of Chicago Press, 1961.

Burr, Aaron. *The Private Journal of Aaron Burr During His Residence of Four Years in Europe with Selections from His Correspondence,* vol. 2. Matthew L. Davis, ed. New York: Harper & Brothers, 1838.

Butler, Marilyn. *Romantics, Rebels, and Reactionaries: English Literature and Its Background, 1760–1830.* New York: Oxford University Press, 1981.

Edelman, Hope. *Motherless Daughters: The Legacy of Loss.* New York: Addison-Wesley, 1994.

Edelman, Hope, ed. *Letters from Motherless Daughters: Words of Courage, Grief, and Healing.* New York: Addison-Wesley, 1995.

Florescu, Radu. *In Search of Frankenstein.* Boston: New York Graphic Society, 1975.

Furst, Lilian R. *Romanticism.* London: Methuen, 1976.

Gilbert, Sandra M., and Susan Gubar. "Horror's Twin: Mary Shelley's Monstrous Eve," in *Mary Shelley.* Harold Bloom, ed. New York: Chelsea House, 1985.

Hogg, Thomas Jefferson. "The Life of Shelley," in *The Life of Percy Bysshe Shelley*, vol. 2. New York: E. P. Dutton, 1923.

Holmes, Richard. *Shelley: The Pursuit.* New York: E. P. Dutton, 1975.

Kiely, Robert. "Frankenstein," in *Mary Shelley.* Harold Bloom, ed. New York: Chelsea House, 1985.

Lowe-Evans, Mary. *Frankenstein: Mary Shelley's Wedding Guest.* New York: Twayne, 1993.

Marshall, Peter H. *William Godwin.* New Haven: Yale University Press, 1984.

Mellor, Anne K. *Mary Shelley: Her Life, Her Fiction, Her Monsters.* London: Methuen, 1988.

Paul, C. Kegan. *William Godwin: His Friends and Contemporaries,* 3 vols. London: Henry S. King & Co., 1876.

Peacock, Thomas Love. "Memoirs of Shelley," in *The Life of Percy Bysshe Shelley,* vol. 2. New York: E. P. Dutton, 1923.

Schwartz, Richard B. *Daily Life in Johnson's London.* Madison: University of Wisconsin Press, 1983.

Shelley, Jane, ed. *Shelley Memorials: From Authentic Sources.* London: Henry S. King & Co., 1875.

Shelley, Mary Wollstonecraft. *Frankenstein, or, The Modern Prometheus.* 1818, rev. 1831. Many editions.

———. *The Journals of Mary Shelley: 1814–1844.* Paula R. Feldman and Diana Scott-Kilvert, eds. Baltimore: John Hopkins University Press, 1987.

———. *Selected Letters of Mary Wollstonecraft Shelley.* Betty T. Bennett, ed. Baltimore: John Hopkins University Press, 1995.

Stone, Lawrence. *The Family, Sex and Marriage in England 1500–1800,* abridg. ed. New York: Harper & Row, 1979.

Spark, Muriel. *Mary Shelley.* New York: E. P. Dutton, 1987.

Stocking, Marion Kingston, ed. *The Clairmont Correspondence: Letters of Claire Clairmont, Charles Clairmont, and Fanny Imlay Godwin,* vols. 1 and 2. Baltimore and London: Johns Hopkins University Press, 1995.

Sunstein, Emily W. *Mary Shelley: Romance and Reality.* Baltimore: Johns Hopkins University Press, 1989.

Tomalin, Claire. *The Life and Death of Mary Wollstonecraft,* rev. ed. London: Penguin, 1992.

Tomalin, Claire. *Shelley and His World.* New York: Scribner's, 1980.

Trelawny, Edward John. "The Recollections of Shelley and Byron," in *The Life of Percy Bysshe Shelley,* vol. 2. New York: E. P. Dutton, 1923.

Index

INDEX

INDEX

About the Author

Joan Kane Nichols has written for young readers for fifteen years. Her books include a biography of Anne Hutchinson and the novels *All But the Right Folks* and *No Room for a Dog.* A lifelong resident of New York City, she is currently writing a murder mystery about Charles Dickens.

THE BARNARD BIOGRAPHY SERIES

The Barnard Biography series expands the universe of heroic women with these profiles. The details of each woman's life may vary, but each was led by a bold spirit and an active intellect to engage her particular world. All have left inspiring legacies that are captured in these biographies.

Barnard College is a selective, independent liberal arts college for women affiliated with Columbia University and located in New York City. Founded in 1889, it was among the pioneers in the crusade to make higher education available to young women. Over the years, its alumnae have become leaders in the fields of public affairs, the arts, literature, and science. Barnard's enduring mission is to provide an environment conducive to inquiry, learning, and expression while also fostering women's abilities, interests, and concerns.

OTHER TITLES IN THE BARNARD BIOGRAPHY SERIES:

Beryl Markham: Never Turn Back
Elizabeth Blackwell: A Doctor's Triumph